F

2020 VISION

Stan Davis
Bill Davidson

A FIRESIDE BOOK
Published by Simon & Schuster
New York London Toronto Sydney Tokyo Singapore

FIRESIDE
Simon & Schuster Building
Rockefeller Center
1230 Avenue of the Americas
New York, New York 10020

First Fireside Edition
FIRESIDE and colophon are registered trademarks
of Simon & Schuster Inc.

Designed by Barbara Marks

Manufactured in the United States of America

1   3   5   7   9   10   8   6   4   2

1   3   5   7   9   10   8   6   4   2   (pbk)

Library of Congress Cataloging-in-Publication Data
Davis, Stanley M.
2020 Vision / Stan Davis and Bill Davidson.
p.   cm.
Includes index.
1. Information technology—Forecasting.
2. Biotechnology—Forecasting. 3. Twenty-first
century—Forecasts.   I. Davidson, William
Harley, date.   II. Title.   III. Title: Twenty
twenty vision.
HC79.I55D38 1991
338′.02′0112—dc20   91-355
CIP

ISBN: 0-671-73237-4
ISBN: 0-671-77815-3 (pbk)

TO

BOBBI DAVIS,

FOR HER

AESTHETICS,

ACCOMPLISHMENTS,

AND

STRENGTH

Contents

A Note on the Chapter Symbols

Because we learn by images as well as by words, each chapter in *2020 Vision* has a graphic, or visual symbol, that represents the key concept and major theme in that chapter. Information is the core of today's economy, and each symbol is also a visual analog of a way in which information profoundly affects all business and their organizations.

 CHAPTER 1: In our economy information comes in four forms and four functions, represented by the interlocking grid, which combine with increasing complexity and sophistication to alter every fact of today's businesses.

 CHAPTER 2: The information in a mature core business, represented by the small white sphere within the larger black sphere, will create the next generation of growth.

 CHAPTER 3: A business turbocharged by information, represented by the white sphere, grows significantly in relation to the company's traditional business, the black sphere, to become an entirely new enterprise.

 CHAPTER 4: Businesses have life cycles and so do their organizations, represented here by overlapping generation curves.

CHAPTER 5: The dominance of core information technologies and industries on a global scale is the essential basis upon which to build future economic leadership.

CHAPTER 6: Today's Information Economy will give way to the next Bio-Economy, represented by the double helix as a dollar sign, the commercialization of genetic engineering technologies which will create new businesses and shape new organizations.

CHAPTER 1

Just Past Growth,
Still Short of Maturity

*I am captivated more by dreams of the
future than by the history of the past.*

Thomas Jefferson

The first time it happens is often in the shower. You catch a glimpse of yourself in the bathroom mirror and unwillingly note the trespass of time. Somewhere in mid-life, instead of thinking how old you are, you begin to wonder how many years you have left.

Wherever and whenever this happens, usually, and meaningfully, we change the way we lead our lives. If we are exquisitely aware that our lives are finite, we are often more tolerant of the little things and focus on what is most important to us. Economies also reach a midpoint in their lives, and clear awareness of our economy's life cycle can have a similarly transforming effect.

Everyone is aware that we are now in what is generally known as an information economy. But the phrase is used so glibly and superficially that it has become almost meaningless. While the information economy began in the mid–1950s, most of us were not even aware of it until the 1970s. For two decades nobody knew we had switched economies. Then, for one more decade a few intellectuals and business visionaries knew and acted, while almost everyone else merely discussed and debated. By the 1980s, there was general agreement that we were in a fundamentally different economy. Still, we debated and discussed and missed opportunities to act on the basis of our insight.

We are now offered a new insight and another opportunity. *This current economy will come to an end in the 2020s, about seven decades after it began. We are already halfway through it.** Thirtysomething and halfway through!

What does this mean? What can we do with this insight? Should we be depressed or energized? Mid-life realizations about both ourselves and our economy are risky opportunities. If we take advantage of these opportunities, they can be

*Principles in this book appear in *italics*

transforming. If we shrug them off, we are unlikely to secure the gains that will make the difference in our personal and collective lives.

With our information economy at mid-life, and recession an ever present concern, the essentials of every business are being altered so fundamentally that you had better not be in the same business five to ten years from now that you are in today. You had better be the first, not the last, to know why, and the first to know what to do about it. If after that short time you are still in the same business, it is likely that you will also be on your way out of business altogether. What's worse, you won't find out until it is too late. Marginal improvements won't be enough to stay competitive. You can get 5, 10, 15 percent improvements in what you are doing by doing the same thing, only a bit better. But your competition will go for improvements in multiples. To attain 100, 300, 500 percent improvements, you can't do the same thing better. You have to do something fundamentally different and, in the process, your business will be fundamentally transformed.

▪ In the Age of Smart Toilets

A clear example of such a transformation can be found in the bathroom fixture business. One of us was in Japan and a tea ceremony was held in his honor at his host's home. Dressed in suit and tie and kneeling shoeless on a tatami mat, waiting for the ceremony to begin, he needed to use the bathroom. He went down the hall in his stocking feet. When finished, he had to press an electronic key pad to operate the fixture. It was all in Japanese. Before he realized what he was doing, he pushed the wrong button and was soaked by the spray from the all-in-one toilet/bottom-washer/bidet!

Japan's leading fixture manufacturer, Toto Ltd., now sells a "paperless" toilet that sprays warm water like a bidet, blows warm air to dry, and even dispenses a scent. "Smart" toilet/bidets are now common in Japan. The machine keeps the seat warm in winter and automatically sanitizes the bowl after each use. In other models, you can control the water pressure, temperature, and angle of the spray. New models analyze urine and measure body temperature, weight, blood pressure, and pulse. More than five million smart units have been sold, and the product is just being introduced into the American market. Bathroom fixtures is a very mature business that has found new growth from the introduction of information into the ceramic core of its products. We are in the age of smart toilets.

Hi-tech, no-touch, automatic bottom-washers have become quite the thing in hygienic Japan. Inax, number two in the Japanese toilet wars, ran a very popular commercial showing a gorilla poking the control panel of a smart toilet, peering into the bowl, and getting squirted by the water jet. This growth in paperless toilets is particularly astounding when you consider that as recently as January 1990, only 40 percent of homes in Japan had public plumbing, and bed pans and outhouses are still common.

Nippon Telegraph & Telephone Public Corporation co-operated in developing a toilet that not only generates information on blood pressure, pulse, temperature, urine, and weight, but also processes, stores, and transmits it. The information can be viewed on a liquid crystal display, which can be located on the unit or on a nearby wall or shelf. The toilet stores up to 130 days' worth of readings, prints them out, transfers them to a personal computer, or transmits them via modem to a medical service for further analysis. At a steep $7,000, the unit's first market will be in health care facilities, and it will enter the home market as the price drops. By the time that happens, the smart toilet will probably be able to differentiate one user's "seatprint" from another's.

American Standard, which also serves the bathroom fixture marketplace, has introduced a smart bathtub in the American market. The bather selects the temperature, humidity, music, air, and water flow with the touch of electronic buttons. The unit has a communications linkage that allows its owner to contact the tub from a remote location and ask it to have the right environment ready at a certain hour. Not only can you operate an office from home, you can now operate your "bathroom environment" from your office.

An important principle lurks in the example of smart Japanese and American bathroom fixtures. Today, *information-based enhancements have become the main avenue to revitalize mature businesses and to transform them into new ones.*

In every economy, the core technology becomes the basis for revitalization and growth. Information technologies are the core for today's economy, and to survive all businesses must *informationalize.*[1] From small mom-and-pop stores to giant global corporations, the point to grasp is not merely that all economic activities will depend upon information to create and control their destiny. We've heard that already. And while it's true, this truth manifests itself so slowly—over decades—that people have tired of it. For many, it is unpoured honey.

Instead of focusing on its not-so-newness, we must focus on the growing power and consequences of this truth. The point is that the economic value from generating, using, and selling information is growing significantly faster than the value added by producing traditional goods and services. Mature businesses will continue, just as do agriculture and industry, but they represent a shrinking proportion of the total economy and require an ever smaller proportion of the economy to meet their resource needs. Increasing the information content of any product or service, to make a smart version of a not-so-smart one, will demand more resource inputs and will yield more productive outputs. All businesses will get increasingly smart, in this sense, or yield to more informationalized competitors.

The value of any product can be increased by incorporating intelligence, information content, and services. Businesses can modernize even their most mature products and services by embedding information features and functions. Increased value does not come from material changes so much as from new intangibles. Choice, variety, and service embedded in traditional products create smart products and new market opportunities.

Profitability from the new features, in fact, often exceeds the profit from the original product or service. *The more information you put into a product, or the more you are able to use a product to pull out information, the more you evolve beyond the original purpose into new ones. These new ones, which are based on information, may present even far greater opportunities than the original.*

■ And We Thought It Was About Playing Ball

Sports teams are a striking example of mature businesses that have spawned new generation, informationalized businesses, whose economic value outstrips that of the original sports. Sports teams used to be thought of as a collection of money-losing tax shelters. Growth today can no longer come from simply playing more games, raising ticket prices, or enticing more people into the stadium. They are managed more like multibillion-dollar entertainment businesses, in which the sports team is the small core around which much larger information businesses are wrapped. For better and for worse, this is a trend that we can expect to find in most businesses as the information economy matures.

The National Basketball Association's business, for example, has almost tripled in the past six years, and NBA franchise values have climbed faster than those of any other major-league sport during the 1980s. The games are the core business, but they are now almost overshadowed by retail licensing, home video, television production, event marketing, publishing, sponsorship, media sales, and other sports-generated information businesses. The average NBA player salary rose to $510,000 in the 1988–89 season, up from $275,000 five years earlier, and the commissioner expects average salaries to reach $1 million in 1993. More sophisticated agents helped, but they had to have market dollars there to bargain for, and these came from information services, not from ball games.

League revenues rose even faster than players' salaries, from $160 million in 1984 to $351 million in 1989, and are predicted to reach $600 million in 1993. Broadcast rights are the largest source of this revenue gain: NBC paid $600 million for four years of NBA basketball, more than triple the cost of the previous contract, and CBS paid $1 billion for seven years of NCAA basketball, more than double the earlier arrangement. These increases reflect the increasing value of the sport's information spin-offs.

The Boston Celtics, for example, are giving new meaning to the phrase "expansion team." In 1986, after their record-winning sixteenth NBA championship, they raised nearly $45 million in a public offering, and became the only professional sports team listed on the New York Stock Exchange. Then they used the money to become a media power, so that they could broadcast Celtics games on their own stations, eliminating middlemen and keeping the advertising revenues. Turner Broadcasting System, owner of Cable News Network (CNN) as well as WTBS, arrived at the same marriage from the other direction, buying the Atlanta Hawks and the Atlanta Braves. The strategy, of course, is only as good as the core product.

Football has had similar spin-off growth, but revenues have not kept up with skyrocketing salaries, and the National Football League experienced a difficult profit crunch. Despite these problems, the NFL signed two four-year deals, one for $900 million with ABC for Monday Night Football at an 80 percent increase, and the other for $450 million with ESPN for Sunday night games at more than double the old price. Newer, more aggressive owners favor revenue expansion to the salary caps preferred by longtime owners, and clearly this will be more in the form of growth-through-information than growth-through-sports. As more homes get cable, for example, pay-per-view television will gear up to let viewers watch any NFL game they want, not just the network game, for the price of a movie ticket. This potential revenue bonanza could threaten the economic balance among teams if revenues are kept according to which teams are watched, and are not shared equally among all teams. If teams are the geese, are their golden eggs packaged information, not the games themselves? We don't think so, but the information game is certainly affecting the ball game more than any other factor.

Baseball is the top revenue-producing professional sport, and it has the broadcast blockbuster of them all. In December 1988, CBS agreed to pay $1.1 billion to major league baseball for four years of exclusive network rights, beginning in 1990. This includes twelve regular-season games, the All-Star Game, both league championship series, and the World Series, which comes to roughly $1 million per inning. The lure is there because one in four American households watches baseball, almost double the prime-time network draw. But networks can lose big as well as win big in the sports event marketplace. ABC profited handsomely, for example, from the $15.5 million it paid for the 1980 Winter Olympics, but is said to have lost around $65 million of the $309 million it paid for the 1988 games.

Baseball, football, basketball, and hockey, in that order the largest money-producing spectator sports, generate around $3 billion. College sports generate almost half of that again. Horse and car racing adds another $1 billion. Golf, tennis, boxing, wrestling, skiing, soccer, and a slew of other spectator activities generate another $1 billion or so, and printed information about all of the above adds $1 billion more. That's between $7 and $8 billion for information-age spectator sports, most of it through broadcasting rather than on-site viewing. On top of that, Americans spend around six times that much on recreational sports. Imagine what new business opportunities are out there for people who discover the information lode in recreational sports!

Both bathroom fixture companies and sports teams are informationalizing their businesses. The former are revitalizing by providing valuable new services, the latter are finding new growth by seeing information itself as a valuable new business. Trends like these are developing in *all* businesses. They occur, not because of shifts in the stock market or in world events, but because of the maturation of this economy's technological base. We have progressed through a sequence of economies, each increasingly developed: from the early hunting and gathering economies, through agricultural and industrial economies, to the current information economy. In each successive economy, enterprises use the core technology to advance their activities. "Bathroom activities," for example, advanced from the bushes to the outhouse, to the water closet and inside plumbing, to the smart toilet. The body-monitoring services in the bathroom of tomorrow show that the technologies of the next economy—the bio-economy—are starting to come on stream.

■ How Do You Know Where You Are in Your Life Cycle?

Economies, and the industries, businesses, and products within them—like people and all other living things—have a *life cycle*. Each behaves differently at different points in its life cycle. Remarkably, however different all these entities are from one another, they all share common characteristics at common life stages.

In the life cycle of an economy, each technological breakthrough produces a subsequent quantum leap in business growth. When the particular technology matures, growth slows. Past mid-life, businesses rely more on marketing techniques and nominal product changes, such as style and colors, to keep their edge. Further advance is marginal, doing the same thing a little bit better. Aging has set in.

Life cycles of economies tend to resemble S-curves, not unlike human life cycles (see Figure 1.1, next page). For each cycle, the first phase is *embryonic*, a gestation period within the framework of the previous economy, like a child born and reared by adults. Although we know that a great deal of growth and differentiation occur during this first phase, from an economic viewpoint the newborn requires enormous investment and does not contribute very much to the overall economy for several decades.

After this relatively long period of gestation and development, a critical take-off point is reached and the new economy enters the *growth* phase, comparable in human terms to early adulthood. This is when our investments begin to pay off handsomely, output accelerates, and returns are high.

Also like people, an economy develops further, into *maturity*. Here, the core sector that gives the economy its name is like the patriarch to all other sectors, the dominant vehicle for creating economic value. In the coming third quarter of our current economic life cycle, information is the patriarch, just as agriculture and industry reigned supreme in previous economies.

In the fourth and final phase, *aging*, vitality and economic results diminish no matter how many resources are pumped into the effort. The aged sectors of a declining economy become very capital intensive and continue to produce their needed output, but contribute only a tiny proportion to the overall current economy. Models for managing and organizing are distinctive contributions of the later years of an economy, only making their appearances like a burst at sunset.

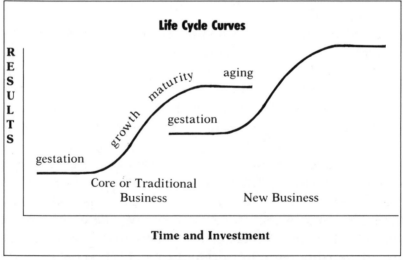

Figure 1.1

Unlike the case with humans, the end of the fourth quarter of an economy does not mean death. It simply means the death of dominance. The sector that lent its name to the economy (agriculture, industry, information) cedes its right to the title

It lives on in the next economy, but only as one of many no-longer-dominant categories.

The beginning of the life cycle curve is characterized by learning and investment, the end by diminishing returns, and the growth and maturity phases in between are generally five times more productive than the aging phase. Usually the life cycle curve is not bell-shaped, dropping back to the economic level where it began. This can happen, however, as in the disappearance of products, as well as civilizations. Technologies, in particular, may be totally eclipsed and disappear forever, as with the galley ship, the crossbow, and the buggy whip. But for the most part, the gains made by one type of economy are sustained, and the next economy's productive ascent builds upon the gains of its predecessors.

The business activities that constitute the infrastructure of an emerging economy climb the life cycle curve first. Once in place, they are followed by all other economic sectors, which build upon the science and technology of the base. When the early industrial base was established, for example, agriculture mechanized, and when the later industrial base developed, it too was succeeded by the industrialization of service delivery. In similar fashion, once the information base of computers and modern communications is fully established, all business activities will follow the infrastructure businesses up the same S-curving path.

If the life cycle for different kinds of businesses were to be plotted on the same graph, we would see a staggered succession of reasonably similar S-curves coming on stream at different times. Financial service businesses, for example, have been among the first to adapt to the new infrastructure, to informationalize. Industrial manufacturing is not far behind. Others, such as publishing, have been slow to adapt and benefit. Even in the age of desktop publishing, from manuscript-in-hand to book-in-store can still take up to one year, and ordering one that is not in the store can still take weeks, if not months.

In general, businesses evolve from an amalgam of technological push and market pull. One is not necessarily more important than the other, but the technology does come earlier. Only with age does technology's dominance pass over to marketing. The market did not express a need for electromagnetism, television, or the telephone. Scientific discovery and technological innovation made them possible, and from the possibilities market demands arose. The core technologies of every economy are the ones that provide the foundation on which the rest of the economy is built. The internal combustion engine and electricity were core technologies in the industrial economy. An understanding of those technologies was necessary to build homes and businesses, and systems of transportation and communication. Information is the core technology of today's economy. Therefore, we need a simple architectural blueprint, a straightforward way to understand all information technology.

■ A Quick Lesson in Mastering the Architecture of Information

Form and function are the essentials of architecture, a distinction made as early as Aristotle. Form and function are widely used to distinguish everything from body parts to auto parts, and it is the interrelation of form and function that often establishes how and why the parts make a whole the way it is.

If we speak of the architecture of information, then, it is useful to look at information in terms of its forms and functions. Form, here, is simply the shape and structure of information, and function refers to the actions or activities performed in its regard. Most information in our economy can be classified into four different forms and four distinct functions (see Figure 1.2). These terms are rather self-evident, and it is very difficult to say much about one without drifting into a discussion of the other. Their power comes from understanding their interplay.

In our economy information comes in four forms: data, text, sound, and image. These forms are all mental impressions that we receive through the senses, and in this economy the senses of sight and hearing are the most important.

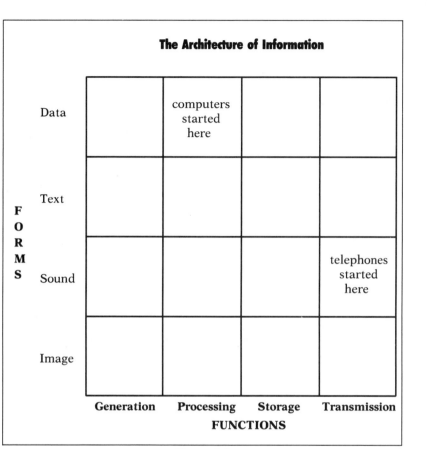

The Architecture of Information

FORMS	Generation	Processing	Storage	Transmission
Data		computers started here		
Text				
Sound				telephones started here
Image				

FUNCTIONS

Figure 1.2

Other forms that information comes in relate to other senses. Taste, touch, and smell, for example, may become important in the bio-economy of the future, but their commercial engineering is many decades away. Other senses, such as intuition and extrasensory perception, are also in their infancy insofar as commercial applications are involved, and they too belong to the next economy, if at all. Neural network computers and artificial intelligence will have to evolve much further before we may even understand the potentials of these senses.

Data are any or all the facts, numbers, letters, symbols, and the like, that can be processed or produced by a computer. Data existed before computers, of course, but it is the computer's unique ability to handle data that led to the information economy itself. When text, sound, and image are reduced to the raw bits of "0"s and "1"s in a computer, they are data. Data, however, most commonly refers to numbers.

Text is written language, to distinguish it from spoken language, which technology treats simply as one form of sound. Text may be written by hand or printed by machine. During the first half of this economy, text meant printed language exclusively. Although handwritten words will never replace the importance of the printed word, they will reappear as useful information in the second half of the economy because machines are learning how to interpret handwriting and transform it into more commonly denominated information. Signatures and handwritten notes, for example, can be machine read and put in print form, or used for identification.

Sound is what we hear, and in this economy we hear basically the sound of voice and music. Radio, telephone, records, and tape recorders are the kinds of products that we use to handle this form of information, and for decades they were very different businesses. The products and their functions, competition, and government regulation were different and did not compete with one another. In today's economy, that is no longer true.

Images are visual forms. They can be photographs or drawings. They can be artistic or practical, realistic or interpretive. They can be presentations or representations, impressions or expressions—as long as they can be seen. Charts and diagrams, faces and landscapes are all images. Some are in black and white, some in colors. The scanned image of a page of text and data is treated as a single image, although new programs have learned to transform them once again. Thus, the copier, fax, printer, and scanner are four separate machines performing essentially similar functions, and therefore likely to merge in the future. In the information economy, however, there are some basic distinctions between still images and moving ones, and between natural images and graphically created ones.

The early decades of our economy produced important

technical and business developments *within* each form of information: from monaural to stereo sound, from black and white to color television, from coldplate to electronic type-setting, from adding machines to calculators. Also, text, data, sound, and image are sometimes translatable into one another. A picture may be worth a thousand words, and made up of a hundred thousand dots. Dots may be numbers, letters, or symbols. Sheet music can be played, translating the dot-like (♪) images into sounds; secretaries take dicta-tion, translating sound into text; and numbers can be used to mean any or all of these forms when the digitized bits are translated into and out of computers. Linkages are con-stantly emerging between and across the forms. Industries that for decades never thought they were related to one another—computers, telecommunications, television, pub-lishing, and so on—began to see the relationship, and with it came a redefinition of who competitors are, or at least would be, in the future. Companies historically as different as AT&T, IBM, CBS, Kodak, Reuters, and Xerox increasingly found themselves in related and competing businesses.

These basic forms of information start to get more com-plex when you realize what can be done with them—their function. Basically, *we do four things with information: gen-erate it, process it, store it, and transmit it.* Anything that is done with any product or service, that deals with any of the four forms of information, can be described in this way. Do-ing one or more of these is what will make the information aspect of business become the most valuable part in the fu-ture.

Generation, the first function, takes information that ex-ists in the environment and captures it for presentation in one of the four forms. An abacus captures the numbers of an accountant and generates a ledger, a typewriter captures the words of an author and generates a book, a recording device captures the sound of a guitar and generates a record or tape, and a photograph captures the image of a landscape and generates a picture.

Generating information, in this economy, doesn't refer to

the creative spark of intellect, but to preparing information to be sent in a form that is easily understood by the receiver. Essentially, this means digitizing it, arranging it into "bits," the basic unit of information with which a computer works. Bits can be magnetized spots, electronic impulses, positively charged magnetic cores, or the like. Once they are digitized, then all *forms* of information can be handled in subsequent *functions* as though they were the same. When photographs are broken down ("read") into digital bits, where each dot in the picture is assigned a value, then pictures can be sent and received by telephone or satellite. Digital audio tape (DAT) does the same thing with sound before it stores it.

Processing, the second function, is where the computer made its first great contribution, starting with data processing, then word processing, and currently voice and image processing, thus covering all forms. The processing function of the computer converts, edits, analyzes, computes, and synthesizes. By the use of semiconductor technology, information is manipulated and transformed. Although today's computers combine generation, processing, and storage, the steps are as distinct as capturing an image on film, developing, enhancing, and enlarging it, then finding a place to keep the information contained in that photograph in intangible form. In the programs they create, software firms generate the rules by which gathered information will be processed.

Storage, the third function, takes information in one of the four forms and keeps it for later use. In the time of the Pharaohs, text and data were stored on tablets, and the Lascaux cave drawings stored images tens of thousands of years before that. Only sound had to wait for the industrial era to be stored on records, tapes and discs. As long lasting as some of these methods of storage are, they are still pretty static because they only capture and hold the information without doing anything else to it. In today's acronymics, that process is called "ROM" for read-only-memory. Storage in an electronic age, however, is dynamic because the storage mechanism is also a processor. A word processor, for example, stores your writing and also lets you retrieve and change it.

Generation and storage are really two sides of the same coin, capturing information.

The storage function is essentially the creation of a "memory bank" where information is filed and collated for later use, and the larger the memory capacity the more information you can store. Books and even whole libraries can be stored by computers, saving vast quantities of space. The story is told of movie mogul Sam Goldwyn, whose files were taking over his office. When he asked his secretary to "get rid of all this," she said, "I can't, some of these are important papers." "All right, then," he said, "make a copy of everything before you throw it out." Today, storage is not only about space but also about making the function active.

Transmission, the fourth information function, comes to us courtesy of the telephone. Simply put, it is the sending and receiving of all forms of information from one point to another, at the speed of electromagnetic waves on coaxial cables, and at the speed of light on fiber optic cables. Whereas storage transfers information across time, transmission moves it across space. It is the distribution function, and includes many activities such as broadcasting, switching, networking, reception, signal processing, collection, and display. While computers dominated the first three functions—generation, processing, and storage—telecommunications has excelled in the fourth function, transmission. More specifically, computers began in the data processing cell and telecommunications began in the sound transmission cell of the information infrastructure.

Simple transmissions, such as by telephone and TV as we used to know them, conveyed voice or images without altering them. The printed word was transmitted in books, newspapers, and magazines in a similarly unaltered way. Modern communications networks, however, add value by combining the other functions together with transmission capabilities. These are the fundamentals of a communications network: many computers all linked together, from big mainframes, through desktop work stations and personal computers, down to the smallest, "dumbest" terminals. The telecommunications linkage is the transmission function. It can occur in any variety of combinations, and can take place within a single building, across the street, or around the world. In telecommunications lingo, there are local area networks (LANs) or wide area networks (WANs).

When networks not only transmit the various forms of information, but also perform the generating, processing, and storing functions, they add enormous value to whatever economic activity is being conducted. Not surprisingly, therefore, they are called value-added networks (VANs).

Most important, transmission can be sent on public and/ or private networks or both. Private networks are more likely to specialize: as in a line dedicated exclusively to fax, or one serving a particular company for all its transmission needs. Public networks are fewer, serve more general needs, take longer to get up and running, and their development and installation has been slowed by government regulation. New investment in private networks in the United States today is outpacing investment in public ones, and this trend is likely to accelerate over the next two decades.

All the combinations and configurations on the form/ function grid produce an endless variety of information-based tools, products, services, and businesses. At a simple product level, for example, attach a tape recorder to a telephone receiver and it stores the sound transmissions. Now we are using three functions and one form. Upgrade to a voice mail system and we can also process the information: listen to messages in any desired order rather than having to listen to them in the order they arrived, send one message to many people, ask to be transferred for further assistance, etc. Four functions, one form. Integrate the capacity to send documents, and even graphic designs, along with the voice message and we are covering all forms and functions. Traditional computing separates form and function in the way software is designed, but new approaches (with the unfortunate name of "object orientation") combine them and make them easier to work with in unison. Combining more forms and more functions equals more added value and more business.

We can go to sound stores now in many cities and "download" any random arrangement of songs we want onto a tape, customized to our own tastes, at little additional cost. Replace the tape with a disc and we upgrade yet again. A disc recorder combines musical sound processing with generation and storage, so that the order of songs, for example, can be moved about. We can also record our own voice onto the sound track of any songs we choose. High tech at low price is creating a whole new market in sound processing and storage, as well as professional quality music recordings that can be produced at home. Developments like these are actually taking place in each portion of the form/function grid.

This simple information grid provides entrepreneurs and managers with a roadmap to the second half of the information economy. Not only can *all* products and services that deal with information be understood in these terms, but also *all* companies can use this grid to build their future businesses on the evolving economic infrastructure. It can be used in three ways. At its simplest, any and all information can be understood in terms of this one conceptual map. Second, if you are confused by all the information vendors and what they have available, or even if you yourself are an information vendor and not confused, it will help you to organize your own information infrastructure and what you might do with it. Third, whatever business you are in, it will become driven by information during the next several decades. So, the better your grasp of information's forms and functions, and the more of them you use, the greater your advantage.

■ Put the Information Infrastructure to Work in Your Company

Infrastructures in any economy are the elementary networks that are put in first, and upon which all subsequent economic activity depends. Real estate developers, for example, first put in the infrastructure of roads, dams, sewage, electricity, and the like, so that communities of homes and businesses can follow. Each economy in history has relied heavily on a particular kind of infrastructure, one that is peculiar to the technology of its era. The railroads, for example, were crucial for the economic development of America in the nineteenth century. The railroad tracks and trains were the infrastructure upon which regional economies were transformed into a single national economy. Railroads were a big business back then, but the multitude of people who traveled on the trains and the businesses that filled the boxcars with products for newly expanding markets became even more important to economic growth.

Similarly, the spectacular growth of the automobile between the 1920s and 1940s prompted the building of the interstate highway network in the 1950s, the infrastructure for the next twenty years of growth. Once again, in consequence, our lives and the economy were transformed. The rapid development of suburbs is just one example. New infrastructures mean economic transformation and subsequent growth. Today, computers, linked by telecommunications, are creating just such a new infrastructure—one might say *"infostructure"*—which will, once again, transform our economy and our way of life. Within one or two decades each of us will possess the full power of the information grid, not only on our desk tops at work, but also in our bathrooms, cars, briefcases, and pockets.

Big businesses and entire industries build each infrastructure, yet their economic value is dwarfed by the even greater productivity of new businesses and new industries that come into being as consequences of the newly laid foundation. In the nineteenth century, for example, very few jobs were created in the manufacture of steam engines. Their importance was not in their own construction, but in the jobs and businesses that their construction subsequently made possible. By the same token, information and telecommunications technologies are very big and very profitable businesses, but the products and services they provide have made many other businesses and industries far more profitable. They have even created new businesses that would have been impossible without the information infrastructure.

In today's economy, many companies have found their

mature businesses adding less and less economic value through time, while related businesses, using the information infrastructure, have begun to sprout up from within the traditional ones and, over the next two decades, will soar. That is why, during bad times, auto companies may make more money off financing cars than from building them, why airlines may make more money from information services, such as reservation systems, than from flying people around, why an auto parts and aerospace company makes almost as much from doing credit checks as from building car and plane parts, why a retailer may make more money from its customer lists than from the clothing and appliances it sells to them, and why a ball club makes less money by playing the game than by selling the video rights. The businesses you were in during the first half of this economy, and before, may not be the ones that will carry you through the second half.

The blending of all forms and functions of information into a single architecture is creating a fundamentally new business economy, but the blending process is being slowed by a number of bottlenecks, technological, economic, and organizational. That, however, is typical of the emergence of new infrastructures. Railroads and highways took decades to build. Although the Wright brothers first flew in 1903, commercial aviation didn't touch the lives of average citizens for over fifty years. It took decades to build the infrastructure of airports, air controllers, travel agents, engine makers, parts suppliers, and reservation systems that support human flight. The refining of oil, which began with a simple distillation process that yielded kerosene, evolved over a period of one hundred years into a complex chemical technology yielding scores of valuable petroleum products. Until the technological blending of telephones, televisions, and computers is accomplished, the infrastructure is not complete, and the economic core, therefore, is not mature enough to develop the truly new models for management and organization.

In the early 1950s, at the beginning of this economy, there were only around four million American households with television, about 10 percent of the total. Halfway through this economy, 98 percent of American homes have television, whereas only about 10 percent have computers. In other words, the computer's presence in our homes is no further along in the early 1990s than was television's presence in the early 1950s. It is quite likely that well before the 2020s, 98 percent of our homes will have computers. Through advanced technology, however, the computer will "look and feel" very much like a television, a hybrid that blends together forms and functions of the architecture of information.

The blending of forms will be largely between the data and text of computers and the sound and image of phones and television. The blending of functions will be largely between the sending and receiving of telecommunications and the generating, processing, and storing work of computers, all of which began to take place mainly during the 1980s, and established the ubiquity of networking. The blending together of all forms and functions may well be the major infrastructure development of the 1990s.

By the fourth quarter of this economy, *in the 2010s, phones, computers, and televisions may be virtually one and the same thing*. That is, phones will process images as readily as they do sound, and computers will process images as readily as they do data. It will be standard for a computer to have a built-in phone, and vice versa. Peel back the picture screen from a television, and every one of them will look like a computer. The "Talking Yellow Pages" is one early example that makes use of the synthesis between telephones and computers. Over the next decade, different products will take partial steps in this direction until ultimate integration is complete.

Picture phones for teleconferencing have already synthesized telephone and television. Today's mainstream video-conferencing technologies cost millions of dollars and require dedicated facilities. But videophoning is closer to your office and living room than you think. Picturetel, a Massachusetts start-up, today provides voice and full-motion video connections over a portable color unit with built-in videocam that looks exactly like a television set, and is about as easy to use. It transmits over leased telephone lines for the same cost as a simple voice call, and connects simply by dialing the other party's telephone number. Each party can control the camera at the other's location, zooming in and out, shifting angles or focusing on documents, charts, or hardware.

Picturetel even permits multi-party conference calls. The product costs about $50,000 today, and each party must have a unit. At that price, it already makes sense for many businesses, especially those with remote domestic or international locations, to use Picturetel for engineering, quality assurance, management reviews, planning, and other meetings. Harris Corporation, in Florida, puts video teleconferencing on personal computer screens for about $20,000 per location. Each system has a personal computer, camera, microphone, video processor, control unit, and software, so that text, spreadsheets, and conversations are handled simultaneously over ordinary telephone lines. The next quantum leap will take this product into your living room. Panasonic offered a home-use product in 1990, at one percent of the Picturetel price, that transmits a new still picture every twenty seconds.

Televisions and computers are also integrating. Many of us already use TV monitors to display video games and computer programs. If a TV can be used as a computer screen, can a computer screen be used as a TV? Nolan Bushnell, the irrepressible entrepreneur and founder of Atari and Chuck E. Cheese Theaters, leads a new firm that brings TV to the computer terminal. Aapps Inc. offers a board that will create a TV screen in a window on a Macintosh terminal. The window will display broadcast TV programs or video programs from a VCR, live camera, or disc player.

Intel plans to take the video-computer linkage one step further. Its new Digital Video Interface (DVI) operates exactly like a text scanner. It captures and stores video images inside a computer. Once stored, these video clips can be edited, manipulated, resequenced, and integrated with other clips. The creative possibilities are endless. Storing full-motion video, however, requires much more space than text.

2020 VISION

A standard compact disc today holds almost fifty thousand pages of text, but only ten minutes of full-motion video. In terms of storage memory, a moving picture is worth more than a thousand words.

The integration of computer and television has often begun with games. The latest crop is what are called "virtual reality" products. These products allow us to control and interact dynamically with video streams. At its simplest, this is a Nintendo "power glove" or a "jump carpet" that drives screen events corresponding to player movements. The player dodges left and the screen figures move accordingly. More sophisticated devices allow the players to control a bird, glider, or balloon in the sky over a selected landscape, for example. The bird dives, glides, or soars with the player's corresponding body movement and the player experiences the result from the bird's perspective on a video screen. Experience this on a large-screen high-definition television, and the impact is unforgettable. Other virtual reality programs allow you to stroll through a selected town at your own pace and direction, to dive coral reefs and ski various mountains. Architects and their clients may walk through their "virtual building" and adjust things as they go: reach out, touch the window, and drag it over a foot or two for a better view; erase a wall here and click in an extra socket there. Consider the possibilities in medicine, recreation, training, travel, and a host of other fields.

Clearly, old businesses are being revitalized and new ones created, but technological bottlenecks in the information infrastructure are currently slowing down its even wider application in our economy. A major reason is that the four forms of information have all been traveling on different tracks. Trains, planes, cars, and tractors are transportation vehicles that run on very different "tracks." Imagine all of them traveling on the same track and you will see bottlenecks, if not chaos. There is no single standard that they will all fit, nor are the existing tracks wide enough to accommodate so much traffic.

The same thing is happening in communications technology. Data, text, sound, and image also travel along different electronic paths. The paths are called bands, and they are not wide enough for all the digitized bits it takes to transmit data, text, sound, and image simultaneously, and as quickly as we want. One bottleneck at this phase of our economy, then, is caused by the only partially met need for compatible computer architectures. Until this is complete, information will run on parallel, rather than integrated, tracks. The other bottleneck stems from the unmet need for virtually infinite bandwidth at nominal cost. But we see openings at the ends of these technological bottlenecks. They are within our grasp.

■ Figuring Out How Many Years the Economy Has Left

The information infrastructure is somewhere between growth and maturity, in the middle of the curve. In much the same way that individuals in the second quarter of life are often torn by their need to choose from among competing life paths, information technology is also offering differing standards to adopt, and the maturation of the infrastructure is stalled by its dilemma of choice. There is a parallel development of technically incompatible mechanisms. IBM, Apple, and DEC, for example, all have developed different proprietary operating structures in their information machines. Telecommunications has had a heritage of single standards, but their standards now vie for dominance with the standards of computers and television. The maturity of the infrastructure may be measured, in part, by the degree to which it adopts standards, develops compatibility among its parts, and connects incompatible pieces into a seamless whole. This process is occurring now and will continue to be *the* major focus during the next decade.

Technologists tell us that infinite bandwidth is here already, and the more business-oriented among them say that meaningful price/performance ratios will be met within about five years. Standards are hotly contested but these also should be in place within the same period of time. Since information technology is evolving faster than its business applications, it is reasonable to assume that the adaptation of these information tools to all businesses in the economy will take even longer. When merged computers/communications technologies are firmly in place, we estimate it will take another five to ten years before all businesses will have been affected the way electricity or automobile technology affected all businesses in the industrial economy.

In the same way that technologies evolve faster than businesses' abilities to absorb them, businesses evolve faster than their managers' abilities to develop new and more suitable organizational forms. That process will take another decade or so and by then the economy will be well advanced into middle age, quite mature. All together, *we can expect capstone managerial models to appear on the scene around twenty years from now*, plus or minus a decade—that is, around 2010—*and certainly not before the end of the century.*

Right now, however, as the information infrastructure shifts from its growth into its maturity, it is very difficult for people to be educated customers. Corporate and retail buyers of the infrastructure tools are understandably reluctant to commit to information technologies and services that might be losers in the standards war. And even if winners are chosen, there is a good chance that they, too, will be technologically obsolete within a decade. Everyone is happy with the advances, yet wishes at the same time that the infrastructure would get through its "thirtysomething" years and settle down into a less turbulent maturity. Once it does, new types of business will become established within all economic sectors, and then we can also expect new types of organizations to run them.

The industrial economy lasted 190 years (the 1760s to the 1950s) globally, and ninety years (the 1860s to the 1950s) in the United States. When in this long industrial economic history did the most widely used model for managing and organizing a company come along? Not until the twilight of the era.

Most executives would give that prize to the model Alfred

Sloan developed at General Motors in the 1920s: decentralized operations around a division structure, combined with centralized planning and financial controls. Second place might go to the distinction between specific activities such as manufacturing and sales, and the management function itself, made by the railroads near the turn of the century. Ford's assembly line and Frederick Taylor's time and motion studies might take third and fourth places. In all instances, these important models did not emerge until the industrial economy was quite mature—for the most part, in its fourth quarter.

We are only three or four decades into the information economy. And it's only for the past ten years that we have been aware of the shift. Now, we know that new models for organizing and managing our businesses are clearly necessary. But if the history of the industrial economy tells managers anything, it is that such new models do not appear until an economy is quite mature. Despite our desires, then, it is unlikely that they will emerge for at least another decade.

This is not cause for alarm or for becoming disheartened. At this point it is still premature to focus on the future organizational models. The last thing a company should want to do is to build an organization prematurely. Only when it knows what kind of business it is going to become will it be able to develop the appropriate and most effective organization.

Allowing for future shock and the quickened pace of change, the information economy will go through its entire life cycle in less time than the industrial economy. It is currently in early middle age and it will come into its own, with its own appropriate economic and organizational models, as it reaches late middle age. If the Sloan model occurred three-fourths of the way through the industrial economy, there is some logic to suggest that 2010, plus or minus a decade, will mark the three-quarter point for the present economy. And it is in the decades after 2020 that the bio-economy will come to dominate while the information economy ages. When we enter the second quarter of the twenty-first century, businesses based on the technologies of the bio-economy will be growing faster than the GNP, while those based on information will have slowed down the way that the manufacturing sector slowed down in the transition from the industrial to the information economy.

■ Now Is Only the Chrysalis of Behemoths

The labor force around 2010 will be made up of today's schoolchildren, for whom computers are not technological puzzles but simply the way things are. Computer visionary Alan Kay has a marvelous definition of technology: it's what wasn't around when you were born. Clothing, paper, and pencils were around, so they're not considered technology. Kay is fond of showing a video of a twenty-two-month-old girl in diapers who is 70 percent literate on the MAC II. She is more dexterous with the mouse than with a pencil, and it is astonishing to watch her turn on the computer, call up an unfinished picture, insert some more lines, put in color, add a title, save and print it, then post it on the refrigerator. Can't you just imagine her older sister showing her a brightly colored box and saying, "They're called crayons. You can use them to generate graphics." The computer is not technology to this generation. Like paper and pencil, it is just part of the environment. This is the generation that will be entering the labor force prepared for new organizational models.

These new managers may very well be led by today's MBA graduates, who average twenty-six years of age. And new organizational models will take shape when this MBA cohort moves into the CEO ranks, in their middle to late forties. Or, just as likely, the budding entrepreneurs who today are building the new information economy businesses will create more important elements of the model than their MBA counterparts. Those who are just beginning their careers as entrepreneurs or as managers may be active participants in the organizational renaissance at the height of their career powers. For those completing their careers before the millennium, this is sometimes received as disappointing news: "I'll be retired by then, so who cares?" Why, then, do mature people plant trees that they will never see fully grown? There is a tremendous job to be done during the coming decade, and it involves very exciting challenges. But they may not be the ones you had hoped for. Astronauts over forty are unlikely to be passengers on the first spaceship to go to Mars, and managers over forty are unlikely to be the ones to create the new models for management in the information age. Today, we can prepare the way—or slow it up. Now is only the chrysalis of behemoths.

We are all acutely aware of the momentous economic changes occurring in the world. We read constantly about whether countries like Germany and Japan will surpass our economic standard of living while we let ourselves slide as Britain has. Are we to put in more than we take out, or will future historians rename ours the spending and consuming economy?

Today, political change is also moving forward with lightning speed and, again, we seem only to follow and lag where once we were the leaders. We are acutely aware that democratic governments and a free society cannot survive for long without a healthy economy. But what must managers and their businesses do to remain healthy, to regain leadership? What use will we make of the time that we have? What is our vision?

This is the moment for asking just such questions, as individuals and as an economy, because both are at mid-life. It is not startling that people, businesses, and the economy all pass through the same seasons of life. It is startling, however, that *the life cycle of the majority of Americans and of this current economy began and will end together.*

■ Two Pigs in the Same Python

Baby boomers, the largest segment of our population, are people born between 1946 and 1964. The information economy began in the early to middle 1950s, smack in the middle of this generation. The life-styles of this generation have been shaped by the electronic and information technologies of the age to create the consumer-based economy we have today. Seventy-seven million baby boomers and the information economy are walking together, step by step, through their respective life cycles, and right now they are both thirty-something, both at the crossroads in mid-life. As a result, large numbers of people are going through life cycle issues that bear a striking resemblance to the life cycle issues of the economy itself. And because demography is much more predictable than economy, it offers a helpful glimpse of both individual and corporate managerial dilemmas.

The causes of this matched pair of life cycles are unrelated, but the effects are not. The information economy began with the aging of the industrial technologies and the birth of new information-based ones. The baby boom began with the return of veterans from World War II and lasted until their generation finished having children. When demographers chart the flow of this generation through time, they describe the big blip on their charts as "a pig moving through a python." As the blip moves into successive life cycle stages, that age group grows about three times as fast as the U.S. population as a whole. The baby boomers are around half of the adult population today, and by 1995 will make up nearly 75 percent of the work force. Their needs, values, abilities, and life-styles will have major impact on the shape and focus of our businesses and our organizations.

Approximately half of the boomers are now between 26 and 35, still part of the young-adult market (18–35) so coveted by business. This is the half that seems to cause optimism. Forty-one percent of those in professional jobs and 37 percent of those in executive, managerial, or administrative positions are in this sub-category. Households are the key consuming unit that businesses pay attention to, and since both the man and the woman work in over three-fourths of the households in this group, their household income is significant: over $50,000 for more than two-thirds of them. They are still acquisitive, driven largely by personal image, and buy most heavily in clothing, hi-tech electronics, home furnishings, recreation, and entertainment. They are imbued with growth-quarter values and behavior, both personally and organizationally. They still see their careers on the rising life cycle slope, and have not yet moved up into the category of the older half of the boomer generation, those 35 to 44, whose growth in career and income will slow down significantly during the 1990s.

It is this older half of the boomer generation that is much more cause for concern. The last of them were born in 1954, just at the creation of the information economy. How have they done? Twenty-five percent of them never made it past high school graduation and another 25 percent never even got that far. Only one in five who were born in 1954 earned a bachelor's degree. This is the educational profile of our labor force. The 20 percent who graduated college are now the leaders and managers of the information economy. What did they study?

For insights into contemporary America, the U. S. Department of Education studied the college transcripts and follow-up questionnaires of over 15,000 members of the high school class of 1972.[2] In preparation for this technological age, 35 percent studied no mathematics and another 30 percent studied the remedial equivalent of high school mathematics. In preparation for this globalized era, only half as many who studied math took any foreign language or international studies courses. Americans ranked last in a nine-country study sponsored by the *National Geographic*, in which 45 percent "did not know where Central America is located, only one-third could find Vietnam on a map, and fewer than half of those tested found the United Kingdom, France, South Africa, or Japan."[3]

By contrast with this relative illiteracy and innumeracy, says the Department of Education study, nearly 30 percent took courses in physical well-being, such as aerobics, jogging, body-building, and yoga. As to life goals, more stressed "having strong friendships" than "the ability to give [one's] children better opportunities." During the second half of this economy, the aging boomers will witness their children's living standards slipping faster than their own, and they will scramble to cover their retiring years.

While experts agree that retirement planning should

have begun by age 40, less than one in four people of this age have begun the process and are accumulating assets at a rapid enough rate to maintain their life-style through retirement. A nationwide Merrill Lynch survey of 45- to 64-year-olds found that only 18 percent save at least 20 percent, even though 74 percent expect the same pre- and post-retirement living standards, and 59 percent want to take early retirement.[4] People will either have to save more, increase the return on savings they already have, accept a lower living standard in retirement, or else postpone it. Not all elements in our 2020 Vision are rosy.

Baby boomers are keeping the Social Security System solvent because they are plentiful. But surpluses are spent elsewhere now, not earmarked for future use when the boomers retire. Moreover, the boomers are being followed by a short generation of baby busters, people who postpone child-rearing until well into their thirties or dispense with it altogether. The result may mean an inadequate population base to fund Social Security in the information economy's final quarter. Between now and then, for example, the ratio of workers to retirees will shift from more than three-to-one to less than two-to-one. At that time, the boom and bust cycles will be followed by what is called the "echo boom," children of the big boom and the work force for the next economy.

■ Are We Up to the Challenge?

This collective picture of us, as people, does not blend particularly well with the challenges our economy faces in its second half. Looking back from the future on the economy's four quarters, we might already imagine these interpretations: nostalgia for our innocence and youthful first quarter (1953 to 1971); optimism and enthusiasm for the growth in the second quarter (1972 to 1990); concern, conservation, and constriction in the maturing third quarter (1991 to 2009); and severe social and economic tensions in the declining fourth quarter (2010 to the 2020s). Avoiding such negative developments will require conscious restructuring of our economic activities, both personal, corporate, and national.

As individuals shift from their growth to their mature quarters, their values and behavior adjust accordingly. Young people often think, "I'll switch to another company unless . . ." Past the mid-career point, they shift to "I'll stay with this company unless . . ." A little later on, they accept less mobility within the same company, spending as much as the last two of their four-decade careers in the same jobs.

A similar progression occurs in businesses as they move into the second half of their life cycles. And as individuals, businesses, and the economy of this country move into maturity, the best way to continue long-term sustained growth is by creating new children, new businesses, and yet another economy for a new generation. *Continuity and growth through successive life cycles.* To date, our business organizations have been slow to adopt this concept. An important sign of economic maturity, in the most positive sense, will be for us to develop models of management and organization that are closely linked to the life cycles of our businesses. Calling a business mature has taken on negative implications. It is thought of as past its prime, its growth slowed, and its future not so grand. Calling individuals mature generally strikes a more positive note. Their health is still good, and supposedly they have accumulated some skills, perspective, and money. We choose to see maturity as prime time for *both* individuals and businesses.

What does it mean to say that during the next two decades our economy will mature? The mature third quarter of the industrial economy covered the latter half of the nineteenth century, and the final fourth quarter spanned the first half of the twentieth. In the United States it was around 1865 before the transition from an agrarian to an industrial economy truly began. The outcome of the Civil War also determined that industrial growth, not farming, would be the basis for the national economy. The industrial sector grew rapidly for many decades thereafter, reaching its largest percent of GNP in 1947, and of employment in 1953. Even though it was mature, there was plenty of dynamism in the second half of the industrial economy, and productivity and living standards soared.

While the industrial economy began in Britain, it nevertheless completed its life cycle in the United States. The United States was the first nation to embark on the new information economy. But will it be the first to complete the current cycle? Or, like the previous economy, will this one begin in one country but end in another? And what will the next economy, which is already in gestation, be like?

Historians tell us that civilizations decline when they overextend themselves, and particularly overmilitarize themselves, on the world stage. The lessons of history abound, from ancient Rome through Germany and Japan in World War II. In the almost half-century since that war, the conquerors have gone into relative decline while the conquered have become victorious through commerce.

Militarist tensions having subsided, both the United States and the Soviet Union are now attempting to redirect their economies. The Soviets are undertaking the more fundamental restructuring, yet the outcome is more certain. No matter how successful they are, they are still unlikely to be meaningfully competitive with American, Asian, or European economies during the next quarter. The people and the government of the United States, by contrast, are not probing as deeply into our own national vision. By the close of the second quarter, even though we find vindication in our model vis-à-vis the Soviets, our world position has nevertheless deteriorated relative to those of the rising commercial powers. Our future, in the third quarter of this economy, is more positive yet more uncertain than theirs.

Despite what Americans would like to believe, we have not been the first to lay the tracks for the new infrastructure of the information economy. The public communications networks in the United States are rapidly falling behind those of its competitors. United States investment, and unconscious yet de facto national strategy, has focused primarily on private, not public networks. The implications of competitive pressures and government policy on the path we have been taking, for the nation, our private businesses, and the average citizen, urgently need attention.

It's time to take that long shower and contemplate the cycles of life. Let the water run a little longer and ask yourself, "Where am I headed? Where is my business headed? And where is my nation headed?"

CHAPTER 2

There Is No
Jack Benny Law of Business—
You Can't Stay 39 Forever

---

*Is it the fashion that discarded fathers
Should have thus little mercy on their
flesh?*

William Shakespeare, **King Lear**, *III.4*

Whether they are tragic or comic, our desires and efforts to invigorate ourselves and our world are very real. King Lear's desperate struggle to hold on drove him to madness and death. On the comic end of the spectrum, when asked how old he was, even toward the end of his life, Jack Benny always deadpanned, "Thirty-nine."

No one and nothing wants to grow old. The struggle to hold on is just as powerful for nations and for businesses as it is for mortals. People and families, businesses and economies, however, all do grow old. There is no Jack Benny law for businesses, and they can't stay thirty-nine forever. What are they to do?

Consider the computer business, a bellwether for the development of all businesses in this economy. It was in its embryonic stage in the 1950s, then burst forth in the 1960s. During the sixties, the focus was on King Hardware, the black box or product. His daughters, Software and Service, were only things you did in order to get the real business. In the beginning, Hardware had the show to himself and everyone bowed to his grandeur. But by the 1970s, his daughters had grown up to become powerful and beautiful young women. As intangibles like operating systems and networking became more important in the computer business, Software and Service vied for equality with their aging father.

The balance of family power shifted irreversibly in the 1980s. Hardware still dominated the revenue figures, but Software and Service came to rule profits. Currently, a typical profile is one in which King Hardware represents around 60 percent of revenues, while the twin Software and Service sisters make up the other 40 percent. But when it comes to what really keeps the family running, the sisters each contribute half of the family profits, and the hardware makers are either bringing in next to nothing or are on the dole. When product technology dominates, its offspring are somewhat dismissively referred to as "aftermarket" stuff. Once they become *the* market, the derogation evaporates. Instead of necessary annoyances that had been treated only as ways to leverage the real business, they became successes in their own right and are now providing the competitive advantage for the future.

The reversal of roles and dominance is no easier to accept in business than in family life. The changes in both are very hard to adjust to. It is a slow process, sometimes taking a decade or more. At this point in time, King Hardware still wants the family culture to reflect his values and beliefs about what is important: "We can only survive and thrive if we bring on the next generation of better boxes." The Service and Software sisters counter with: "Your boxes are commodities that our customers can buy anywhere. Customer-focused marketing is a truer path to the future than your technological one." And as in most family arguments, each is right in a different way, and the family can only survive by valuing both contributions.

This little parable is not restricted to the computer business, and the point is not only that firms can revitalize themselves by promoting younger-generation products and businesses. Information technology can be applied to revitalize *existing* products and businesses. You have already seen how information capabilities can be imbedded in hardware, creating smart products. The larger point is that *when you change dramatically how the business is conducted you transform the business itself. Changes in information technology* are doing just that to every enterprise in the economy. When the technological means for conducting a business change sufficiently, the resulting business is itself transformed, and how you manage it has to adjust accordingly. Information technology has not simply added another function to the way businesses are conducted. It has altered the process so radically that the very nature of businesses and, accordingly, the way they are managed and organized are fundamentally altered.

Mature businesses are utilizing information technology, first to survive, and then to thrive. Like the sons and daughters in a family, *information is a survival tool to older-generation businesses.* In families it can be tragic when the elder generation cannot see the younger players coming into their own and refuses to pass on power to the next generation. Avoiding the same tragedy in business means that traditional enterprises must enthusiastically raise these enterprising offspring and come to see information itself as the successor to their thrones. If they can do this, besides ensuring the next generation of their businesses, in the process they will also extend their own robustness and longevity. The airline, automobile, and clothing industries are all attempting this, each in its own particular way.

■ Three Tales of Life After Forty

Airlines Ever since deregulation, it seems that airlines have been going through a hard time, fighting unions, takeovers, terrorism, competition, and a host of other worrisome, if less lethal, problems. But one significant place where airlines are looking to overcome these obstacles and to find a competitive edge is in the information dimension of their business.

Most people know, for example, how American Airlines' Sabre reservations system became an early "new generation" hero. Sabre began as an efficiency move, until management saw its larger potential to make money as a valuable service to all airlines and their customers, and to American in particular. Based on its evaluation at the time of the blocked 1989 attempt to merge with Delta's Datas II reservations system, Sabre was worth more than $1 billion, or 25 percent of American Airlines.

Despite its brilliance, however, Sabre is built more around the company's needs than the customer's. The system can tell you how many seats are available on a plane, for example, but it cannot tell you if this is a passenger's first or fiftieth flight on a given route. It also cannot analyze the needs of a particular traveler and customize services accordingly. Sabre has not yet informationalized for the customer.

The potential exists for informationalizing all aspects of

the airline industry, particularly where the customer is involved. Canadian Airlines International is taking just this approach. There are three places where it comes into contact with all its customers: in the distribution channels, in the airport, and on the airplane. An airplane captures information about its customers primarily from the first of these. But *companies that capture and utilize information at each point of contact with customers will be better off than those that do so at only one or a few points.* An airline that also captures information about customers in the terminal and on the planes will be able to run more efficiently and to serve customers better than those who capture information about them only through the distribution channels. Each point of contact can be informationalized to improve customer service and operating efficiency.

Distribution Channels Direct access to computerized reservation and ticketing services will grow in popularity through easy-to-use retail services similar to Sabre. Self-ticketing eliminates manual paper processing and overhead, providing operating efficiencies in distribution. Customers will design their own flight packages, including seating, dining, and other options. This builds customer profiles, which can be used in multiple ways. Car and hotel linkages can be offered and arranged. The customer data base can be used to forge marketing joint ventures. When you use a Citibank/ American Airlines Visa card, for example, you earn a mile for every dollar spent, and both companies build their customer data-base profile, purchase by purchase.

Airports After capturing and processing all that customer information in the marketing activity, the next informationalizing takes place in the airport. Just as banks and fast food businesses have gained efficiencies with electronic self-service, airlines can do the same by initiating self-serve check-in. Bar code and electronic tracking will lead to assured baggage handling that will not only keep track of luggage but also initiate corrective actions *before* angry passengers have to do so after they have discovered their luggage is missing. As with a Federal Express package, absolutely, positively assured baggage delivery is a value-added airport service. Once developed, self-serve technology, assured baggage delivery, and other such services will have potential as new businesses for sale throughout the industry. And imagine a service that gives exact and accurate arrival and departure information, not only on screens in the airport but through telephone or terminal connections, anywhere. That may stop some of us from running red lights as we race to a flight that's two hours late. These are the types of services that will develop in the information economy's mature quarter.

Airplanes   The third customer contact point, and hence another place to informationalize, is on the airplane. The basic vehicle is an on-board computer, serving both customer (leisure and business passengers), crew (pilots and flight attendants), and ground operations (maintenance, baggage handlers, caterers) as a multi-purpose network. The on-board information network is targeted at all three benefits: better costs and controls, better service, and new business opportunities.

Data-capture on board, for example, would eliminate overhead and inaccuracies from the verbal or paper methods currently used for crew payroll (flight times), fueling, catering, passenger counts, and so on. There are important operating efficiencies to be had from a "paperless aircraft."

The on-board computer can assist and entertain passengers who are generally locked into their seats. Currently, sound is piped into each seat on planes, and passengers have up to twelve listening choices. But when viewing is available, they must all watch the same screen, with no choice. Video screens will be installed in individual seats during the next decade, the same way sound systems were, and passengers will be able to make much more productive or entertaining use of their time. Touch-tone screens will keep it simple. Passengers will have several choices of entertainment, shopping, business, and educational programs. Imagine in-flight electronic bridge, bingo, and "sky lotteries." And with next-generation, satellite-based sky phone services, air-to-ground communications will expand to its full potential, permitting two-way voice, data, text, and eventually video connections. The basic logic is that while passengers are captive in flight, apart from more edible meals, the best way to keep people occupied is through information.

The sale of airline support services, such as performing suppliers' invoicing and selling weather information, and also direct marketing and advertising targeted to passengers, are new on-board business opportunities. A prototype could be designed and built in a joint venture, say with companies like IBM and Boeing, which could also seek participation from seatback vendors, galley manufacturers, and caterers. Informationalizing an airline would achieve all three benefits of saving money, adding services, and launching new businesses and can take place at the three main points of contact with customers—on the airplane, at the airport, and in the distribution channels.

This broad framework, applied here to an airline, can be used to structure the informationalizing of any business. The approach rests on the belief that any business activity can be improved through the application of new business methods and technologies. The initial benefits appear in the form of internal operating efficiencies. With refinement and extension, a wave of value-added services can be offered to the customer, differentiating the vendor from traditional competitors. Finally, the new operations and services can break away and become a free-standing business that can ultimately grow to rival or surpass the original business in revenues, profits, and market value. At that point, the focus shifts from informationalizing an existing business to operating and managing new info-businesses.

These three benefits tend to occur in sequence, beginning with internal operating efficiencies and adding enhanced services that can become stand-alone businesses. Firms with new info-businesses typically have passed through the earlier phases of informationalization. Companies generally feel that they need better internal efficiencies when they are in trouble, feeling competitive pressures, narrowing margins, slowed growth, and the like. Once their own house is in order, spreading the advantages of informationalized management externally, to customers, is the logical next step. They begin by modifying their existing operations, and end up with an entirely new business. Some very customer-oriented firms, on the other hand, begin informationalizing at their points of customer contact, and address internal concerns only later. This, however, is unusual because it is difficult to deliver excellent customer service when your internal operations are not excellent themselves.

Automobiles   The automobile industry today is using information technology in very different ways. General Motors was the ultimate organization of the industrial economy, while now many question its ability to survive to the end of the information economy. G.M., of course, would like to be a leading competitor in the new economy rather than just survive, and its use of information is playing a vital role in that attempt.

Despite G.M.'s slowness to adapt, its average car today already contains as much information-processing power as was on board the Apollo moonlanding craft in 1969, and more than a 1970s mainframe. Informationalizing, however, means more than producing smarter cars. It begins before the car is built. G.M.'s Buick Division offers a system, for example, that allows customers to self-design highly customized car configurations on terminals in their dealers' showrooms. Customers select the body, suspension, engine, tires, color, interior, and other specifics from a large number of options. The vehicle takes form and changes before their eyes. Every element is open to a range of pre-engineered options, and the vehicle price is calculated in real time for each evolving configuration. There are already software packages that simulate test drives of any vehicle configuration. The ability to examine, in advance, the result of any customized product selection is one of the informationalized features that G.M. is depending on to secure customer acceptance.

When the customer-cum-designer is satisfied and ready to place the order, the dealer conducts an immediate electronic credit analysis and assists in establishing a financing package. All of this, too, is done instantaneously at the dealer's terminal. Once the selections have been made, the dealer pushes the send button, electronically entering the customized vehicle order into G.M.'s production schedule. Each order will trigger electronic requests from predetermined suppliers for the precise parts and components needed to produce that exact vehicle.

Today only about 5 percent of new car buyers actually place a custom order. The rest buy off the lot. Car makers say that they can custom order, produce, and deliver a car within eight weeks, although many customers report waits of six months or longer. The Buick production complex in Flint, Michigan, the trial site for these developments, is currently operating on a ten-day production schedule. Normal supplier response times in the plant range from less than an hour to no more than sixteen hours. Thus, it is conceivable that standard-priced customized vehicles can be mass produced within as little as two weeks. A friend recently reported that he ordered a custom vehicle from Detroit on Monday and drove it home Thursday of the same week. The car was produced on Tuesday, shipped on Wednesday, serviced on Thursday, and in his garage in Toronto that evening. When a custom car can be produced and delivered in one week, it is likely to alter buying behavior. Would you like to design your own car? How about your teenage son?

Unit costs for customized, on-demand cars need not exceed costs for standard vehicles. G.M. is already producing countless auto configurations. Using traditional business logic, it pre-manufactures those vehicles in anticipation of customer demand, and holds them in inventory while waiting for the order. With on-demand manufacturing, units are not produced until they are ordered. The pink Cadillac convertible desired by the new punk rock star in Los Angeles doesn't have to be pre-manufactured and held in inventory on a lot in Miami.

The difference in cost between on-demand and pre-demand manufacturing for the entire industry is represented by over $50 billion in finished goods inventory around the world. Domestic and foreign auto stocks typically exceed seventy-five days' worth of sales. The opportunity to shrink inventory holds immense potential in this industry and in others. Those savings will more than offset the costs to informationalize the business, and that means that customized vehicles can be produced at little or no extra cost.

The G.M. concept sounds good, but how quickly and effectively can it be implemented? Perhaps not quickly enough. The production schedule in Toyota City is now three days. While Toyota does not offer as many options as G.M., it is nevertheless possible to order a customized car in Japan on Monday morning and drive it away that Friday afternoon. The informationalized car business is a far cry from the Toyota of just a few short years ago, which produced standard vehicles with literally no factory options on sixty-day fixed production schedules. Other Japanese motor companies are catching on to the new logic as well. Hino Motors, a Japanese leader in the truck industry, can now produce over 1,900 different types of trucks with an average lead time of just five days.

Dramatic changes in operations are required to provide such rapid response to customized orders. Even more profound shifts in supplier links are required. At Toyota, when a dealer places an order for a specific vehicle, the order goes directly into Toyota's production schedule. Toyota does not then place orders for the required parts, because its suppliers automatically check the production schedule and deliver the required mix and quantity as needed. In turn, the suppliers do not bill Toyota for their deliveries. Toyota simply reviews its production schedule to determine the amount it owes each supplier. Order entry, fulfillment, and payment not only occur with minimal delay, but with minimal overhead. Informationalized businesses like Toyota experience dramatic reductions in traditional overhead functions and costs.

To design, produce, deliver, and also finance products in real time requires that all links in the business chain be tied very closely together. Suppliers, manufacturers, distributors, and retailers may still exist as independent companies, but the interdependencies among them become so total that the concept of an arm's-length relationship may disappear completely. Intimate electronic linkages to independent parties typify informationalized firms, but fly in the face of past auto industry practice.

The U.S. auto industry generally has not allowed any vendor to supply more than 50 percent of a car maker's needs for any component. Rigorous, lengthy, and contractual purchasing negotiations are common. Multiple suppliers were the rule, and automakers often played suppliers off against each other for price and other concessions. Those old practices and relationships are now being displaced by new electronic relationships.

Despite its many problems, G.M. does understand the kind of electronic infrastructure it needs to survive into the next century. It acquired EDS, the largest independent vendor of information networks, to build it. G.M. accounts for 50 percent of EDS revenues, or almost $3 billion per year. If you want to do business with G.M. today, you had better be on the EDS network. Moreover, the network that links G.M. to its suppliers and dealers is changing how it operates more dramatically than it is changing what it produces. Among other things, this means embracing a world of customer self-design, mass customization, rapid response, on-demand manufacture, zero inventory, and closely-coupled relationships that are held together electronically.

Networking and its electronic implementation may well be the most important element of business strategy in the next decade, and it is nowhere more evident than in the automotive industry. Networking is simply the set of relationships you create and maintain, in this case with suppliers, allies, distributors, and customers, to manufacture and market your product. It has always been central to business strategy, but electronic networking elevates the importance of planning how to use information technology. Your profile of electronic capabilities—including hardware, software, communications, data formats, and other infrastructure elements—increasingly will drive business performance by determining with whom you can link. Buyers increasingly will shun suppliers who do not offer electronic linkages, or who have inaccessible information systems.

In the industrial economy if you built a better car, mousetrap, or whatever, the world beat a path to your door. Today, the game has shifted to building a better path. Whoever owns the information pathways, the vital connecting links, will call the shots. Furthermore, it is critical to be on the right path because electronic connections require compatible infrastructures. What if G.M., Ford, and Toyota, for example, all utilize dramatically different computer and communications standards? It isn't just a question of different protocols. All aspects of operations must be aligned. Electronic integration, therefore, may lead to the clustering of firms with common electronic pathways.

The Japanese call clusters of companies that orbit around core financial and industrial enterprises *keiretsu* groups. Mitsubishi, the largest *keiretsu* group, consists of an inner circle of twenty-eight companies reporting annual sales in excess of $300 billion. These companies are surrounded by a galaxy of thousands of other manufacturers, suppliers, distributors, and affiliates. In 1986, the Mitsubishi *Kinyo Kai*, or management council, created a committee of representatives from the core companies to plan an information infrastructure for the group. The resulting Mitsubishi International Data Network (MIND) project is a $20 billion effort to deploy a global network linking all Mitsubishi affiliates, customers, and suppliers. MIND has become the vehicle for all transactions in the extended Mitsubishi family. G.M. is also striving to become an electronic *keiretsu*.

Envision leagues of companies bound together around common infrastructures, leagues that are separated from each other by barriers of electronic incompatibility. Informationalized activities within these groups will offer dramatic benefits relative to transactions between traditional, pre-informationalized firms or between groups with incompatible networks. Network efforts such as those at G.M. and Mitsubishi are under way in giant enterprises throughout Asia, Europe, and the United States. Business velocity, efficiency, and precision within these groups, fueled by informationalized transactions and relationships, will rise sharply as the information economy matures.

Clothing The apparel industry, like airlines and cars, is also being revolutionized by the new business methods. The clothing industry is basically a five-link chain: fiber → fabric → apparel → outlet → consumer. DuPont makes fiber, for example, Milliken and J. P. Stevens turn it into fabric, Levi Strauss makes it into clothing, and J. C. Penney sells it to the consumer. Making the fiber, then the cloth, cutting and stitching it into garments, and getting it onto the retailer's shelves and into customers' hands normally requires a sixty-six-week cycle!

Even if a retailer spots a trend immediately, by the time it gets the goods, the trend can easily be past. Store buyers have to make judgments a year in advance about styles, colors, and sizes. With such long lead times, it is hazardous at best to forecast demand patterns, economic and weather conditions, and fashion and style trends. A wrong guess results in huge losses, both from stock-outs on popular items and from markdowns on slow-selling goods. In this pre-informationalized pattern, the best time for consumers to buy winter clothes is always in April, during the end-of-season clearances when prices are slashed 50 percent or more. Having the right goods in real time would revolutionize apparel retailing.

Industry experts concur that only eleven of the sixty-six weeks in the clothing delivery cycle are spent actually adding value to the garment. The rest of the time is lost in inventory—waiting in process, in transit, or on warehouse shelves. Industry consultant Kurt Salmon estimates that forced markdowns, lost sales, and inventory costs account for as much as 25 percent of the $100 billion-a-year U.S. apparel industry. Twenty to twenty-five cents of every dollar we spend for clothing, groceries, automobiles, and other consumer durables probably gets squandered needlessly in distribution systems that were built for the industrial economy we left over three decades ago. Informationalize!

As many as forty-five of the fifty-five-week supply pipeline in the apparel industry could be eliminated by informationalizing what is often called "quick response" or "rapid response." The result would be big savings for customers, bigger margins for providers, and a narrowing cost gap between domestic and foreign suppliers. With shorter lead times, forecasting accuracy rises sharply and the ability to fine-tune inventory positions reduces stock-outs and clearances. Retailers such as Wal-Mart, J. C. Penney, and Sears are getting the message through to suppliers: informationalize or find new outlets for your goods. Let's see how this is being done.

Levi Strauss is one company working to quicken its response, through its Levilink system, which includes seven services to retailers. Electronic purchase orders help reduce order entry time and vendor marking eliminates the need for in-store ticketing. Other services include bar-coded carton tags for expediting shipment, electronic packing slips to speed unloading, and electronic invoicing.

Further up the chain, new systems measure, color code, and inspect fabric as it comes off the loom, so that it can go directly from the delivery truck to the cutting room when it reaches the apparel factory. This cuts layers of both management and labor, with significant overhead savings. But time is the key factor in the equation. Executives, used to worrying about the time value of money, now have to manage the money value of time. It works for Levi Strauss. With its new services, the company reduced its average order response time from three months to less than one week.

A larger industry-wide effort is under way, developed by the American Textile Manufacturers Association, to create an electronic network connecting all layers in the chain. Retailers order specific garments through terminals that simultaneously trigger orders up the chain to specific apparel, fabric, and fiber companies. In the initial trials of this new system, the procurement cycle was reduced by almost 90 percent and inventory by 65 percent. Order processing and logistical costs were cut by 60 percent, and retail profits increased by as much as several hundred percent, as stock-outs and markdowns were cut sharply. Will we see the ultimate extreme of self-designed, customized clothing that is instantaneously mass-produced and mass-delivered to individuals everywhere? We do not see this happening between now and 2020. The combined forms and functions of information, however, do establish new parameters for success. Information networks, plus computer-aided design, flexible cutting and sewing gear, robots that can handle draped fabric, just-in-time delivery, and a host of other new business methods are helping the clothing industry catch up with pioneers in other industries.

What is happening in the airline, car, and clothing industries shows us what will happen to most business relationships in the years ahead. Different industries will figure out how to informationalize at different paces, but just as they all industrialized, they will all eventually informationalize. But while this is true for industries, not all individual companies will make the transition. Many will not survive because they will fail to reconfigure their businesses around the new operating technologies and principles. Old standards of service, precision, speed, and efficiency simply will not make the cut in the new economy. Customers will shun those firms that have not built the capacity to informationalize their operations. Competitive advantage and business growth belong to those firms that write off already obsolete operations and orientations and move forward to establish new standards of performance.

These trends are becoming more and more apparent. They are not isolated events; each leads logically to most of the others, depending on your particular business. Taken together, a number of equations emerge that present a coherent picture of how mature companies will behave in the second half of the economy.

■ Informationalization = Customized Products + Rapid Response

In any period, a few businesses pioneer a new method or approach that gives them a decided advantage. Competitors and admirers rush to embrace the new methods and a consensus is achieved. But after a time, they no longer provide the desired competitive edge; they are necessary, and no longer sufficient. If they then become conventional wisdom, they harden into biases and blind us to seeing things in other ways. If they are, and have been, perennial truths, the task is to remain true to their thrust while also adding new insights. Quality, productivity, and customer service were the perennial truths of the 1980s. They remain crucial to success, while others are now joining their ranks. *The ability to mass customize, which includes self-design, and to operate in real time, which means rapid response, are becoming permanent fixtures.* Here are some examples of their applications:

Home Mortgages   A friend recently went through the tortuous ordeal of applying for a home mortgage. He was sixty-three days into the mortgage application review and approval process when the bank required extensive financial documentation that involved several thousand dollars' worth of accounting fees. The purchase had to be postponed and the home could have been sold to another buyer because of the bank's inability to issue the mortgage within the escrow period prescribed in the purchase contract.

While the traditional home mortgage industry is still torturing its customer base, other lenders are stepping forward to do the job in minutes. A TV commercial by Direct Trust, in Toronto, begins with a customer's phone call:

Customer: "Hello, is this Direct Pizza?"
Company: "No, this is Direct Trust."
Customer: "Well, what do you sell?"
Company: "We sell home loans, personal loans, and other financial services."
Customer: "How long would it take you to get me a home mortgage?"
Company: "Oh, about fifteen minutes"
Customer: "I can't even get a pizza that quickly!"
Company: "We'll be glad to take your application and approve your loan within fifteen minutes."
Customer: "If it takes longer than fifteen minutes, do I get it free?"

Tag line: "If you would like to try this home loan by phone service call (###) ###-SAVE."

People are not going to stand in line for forty-five days for a standard mortgage if someone will give them a customized, hassle-free home loan in a matter of minutes.

Insurance Claims　The auto insurance industry views claims as a necessary evil. Internal standards are set to keep operating costs to a minimum, and settlements are thought to be fair if neither the adjustor nor the recipient is satisfied. Customer service is often a foreign concept. To tackle these problems, Progressive Insurance has been experimenting with an "office van." The van includes a PC with modem, printer, fax, and two cellular phones, together with soft chairs and refreshments. It is a complete office operating out of a roving mobile van, capable of appearing on the scene of an accident within fifteen minutes and settling the claim—including payment—within an hour and a half maximum. When physical injury is not involved, the insured is invited into the van and offered a soft drink while the report is filed and verified, and a check is issued on the spot. This simultaneously cuts down on office expenses, tow charges, and storage, eliminates additional expenses incurred by lawyer involvement, and increases customer satisfaction. The results, so far, have been encouraging and Progressive would like their vans to become as familiar as UPS trucks and Federal Express vans.

Magazines and Books　*Time* magazine has published East and West Coast editions for some years. It now publishes a different version of its magazine for different parts of Los Angeles. In the spring of 1990, *Time* initiated a new program that distinguishes specific market segments, such as families with children under four years old, and affluent heads of households over fifty years of age, for example. These subsegments will receive specific versions of *Time* containing articles and advertisements tailored to that market. *Time* showed off its customizing capabilities in its November 26, 1990, issue by displaying each individual subscriber's name on his cover, as an opening for an article on the new world of direct marketing.

Such customized magazines require new-age printing services. R. R. Donnelly, *Time*'s principle printer, is the largest printing company in the world, and also one of the oldest and most profitable. It uses its electronic binding technology to mass-customize magazines and books. When *Farm Journal* fell upon hard times in the mid-1980s, subscriptions fell sharply and bankruptcy was a very real prospect. Its 890,000 subscribers included 62,000 hog farmers, 5,000 wheat farmers, and so on. Donnelly's technology allowed the *Farm Journal*, its first customer for this service, to include sections on pigs for one set of its readers, articles on wheat for another segment, and to tailor advertising content to specific segments accordingly, while retaining the benefits of discount postage for mass mailings. As a result, three neighboring farms might receive very different versions of *Farm Journal*, but each would have an advertisement for John Deere tractors citing the local dealer. Advertisers, now able to target their offerings to specific segments with the greatest potential interest in their products, responded enthusiastically to the change. *Farm Journal* today carries a market value in excess of $250 million.

These new capabilities are also spreading to academia. In a joint venture launched in 1989, McGraw-Hill, Eastman Kodak, and R. R. Donnelly announced a new service that allows educators to assemble customized textbooks. These textbooks can contain any combination of copyrighted articles and instructor's materials in the sequence desired by the buyer, and they can be printed and shipped directly in weeks, thus bypassing the antiquated distribution channels. A clearing house for royalty payments to publishers and authors supports this new service.

Semiconductors   The logic for custom chips is powerful. Custom chips occupy less space, require less power, cooling, assembly, and packaging, and cost less. For those reasons, Network Systems of Minnesota replaced two full circuit boards in a terminal connection device with a single customized chip. The cost dropped from over $300 to less than $100. When Apple redesigned the Apple II line from standard to custom chips, it reduced 117 individual standard chips to four custom circuits, reducing unit costs by almost 50 percent.

IBM has operated a quick turnaround time (QTAT) facility for custom semiconductors for over a decade. At places like Sindelfingen, Germany, La Gaude, France, and Fujisawa, Japan, its engineers create custom chip designs using standard computer-aided design (CAD) software. The designs are transmitted electronically to East Fishkill, New York, for prototype production, and the finished chips are air-expressed back in an average of two weeks. Initially, the customer was an internal employee. The next logical extension will link the custom design capability directly to customers in the marketplace. VLSI Technologies Inc. (VTI), to cite another example, uses a communications network for customers to design and transmit advanced microcircuit specifications from their own locations directly into VTI's production schedule.

Pagers Motorola's pager division sales force carries portable computers in the field that allow customers to design a pager to their own specifications. Those specs are communicated via modem and public telephone lines to the pager factory at Boynton Beach, Florida, where the first unit can be produced and shipped in as little as two hours. In all, the factory is capable of producing over twenty million pre-engineered pager types in accordance with customer specifications. This new logic will not be limited to pagers. Centralized production combined with the rapid delivery of customized products designed by customers in their own locations will become common in most businesses. Imagine designing and ordering a new pager, or any other "thingamajig," today and having it in your pocket tomorrow morning.

Checkbooks Checks are a primitive form of funds transfer, one step up from cash exchange, and two up from barter. Many predicted that checks would disappear in the information economy, but Deluxe Corporation continues to produce checkbooks, while posting double-digit growth rates and return on equity in excess of 20 percent per year. The profits and growth come from adding speed to customized design. They have informationalized check printing.

Each of the millions of checkbook orders Deluxe receives every month requires a different name and address, and a

.unique combination of size, color, layout, picture, stub, binder, print style, and format. Even so, Deluxe ships all of its orders within twenty-four hours of receipt. Providing electronic design terminals in bank offices would eliminate the time lag in the ordering process. Customers then could make selections, preview facsimiles of the finished product, and transmit their order instantly into Deluxe's production line, dramatically reducing front-end delays.

■ Informationalization = Manufacture at Point of Delivery

In the pager and check businesses, centralized production is consistent with informationalization. But another way of accomplishing rapid response to customers is to move the final production stages as close to the customer as possible. Could checkbooks be produced in the same location where they are designed? Printing and film processing have already moved production into the retail outlet, and other businesses will follow. The traditional factory is disappearing in many businesses, and manufacture is moving down into the distribution and delivery systems. Here are two examples of businesses in which this has already happened.

Eyeglasses Eyeglass lenses used to be made, stocked, and ground in some central location, and retail outlets would order them to fit frames their customers had picked. Delivery took weeks. Today, it takes about an hour. Lenscrafter stores are fully integrated businesses combining design, production, and delivery. Each customer gets a full visual diagnosis, a precise and unique lens prescription, and the lenses are ground, polished, and fitted to the chosen frame on site, within one hour. Lenscrafter, with 305 stores in 1989, is the most profitable division of U.S. Shoe Corporation, a footwear and specialty retailer that is attempting to rejuvenate mature businesses by applying the principles of the information economy.

Pizzas Lenscrafter moved the factory to the retail outlet. It's possible to get even closer. Pizzas, for example, used to be made in the back of the shop and eaten in the front. Home delivery, the fastest growing segment in the pizza business, eliminated the need for the front of the store. Now, pizzas are cooked in the delivery truck, eliminating much of the need for the back of the store as well, and the pies come directly from the mobile oven to your table.

The production center and retail outlets of the pizza business have yielded their importance, and even their existence, to the information center and the distribution system as key elements of the informationalized pizza business. This will happen to many more businesses during the coming decade: a central information center, which may be located anywhere with an 800 or 900 number, will direct orders to distribution and delivery channels where the final manufacture will take place.

A growing variety of goods and services will be designed, bought, and delivered directly to the home, bypassing retail outlets. Traditional retail outlets will continue to lose share to mail-order and more advanced shop-at-home services. These services will offer increasingly sophisticated video window shopping, self-design capability, greater variety, twenty-four-hour-a-day service, and fast delivery. These new services will remove layers of agents and intermediaries, not add them.

The core function in each economy moves further down the value chain as that economy matures. It was the supply of raw materials in hunting and gathering economies. Agriculture guaranteed their supply, and today that mature function is called purchasing. Production was the core of the industrial economy. The key function moved to marketing with the emergence of the information economy. During the first half it was focused on the marketing mix of pricing, packaging, and positioning. In the second half, *the key function is moving again, into distribution and delivery*.

■ Informationalization = Shrinking Overhead, Inventory, and Working Capital

The growth of informationalized business relationships is fueled in part by benefits derived from the reduction of overhead and working capital. The opportunity to shrink working capital is immense. Preproduction of standard products, in large-scale facilities remote from customers, with stockpiling of inventory, is now a way of the past.

In the information economy, finished goods inventory will fade rapidly, and most goods and services will be designed, produced, and delivered to order with minimal delays. As the need to hold inventory shrinks, working capital will decline as a portion of all enterprise balance sheets. Different assets, such as data bases and network nodes, will replace them, and current accounting techniques will have to recognize these new realities.

The informationalizing of payment methods will also shrink working capital. In today's typical business transactions, a customer sifts through a variety of sources to choose a product and vendor, then completes an order and gives it to the vendor. The vendor processes the order and ultimately ships the product. A short while later, the vendor mails an invoice to the customer. The invoice goes to the customer's payables department where, after a suitable time interval and assuming no complications, a check is cut and mailed. The vendor's receivables department processes the check and mails it to the bank. The bank receives and processes the check and ships it to the clearing bank, which ultimately transfers funds that will be credited to the vendor's account. That process, initiated millions of times a day in the United States and around the world, is how we still do most business today. Our children will think of us as incredibly primitive.

There is a better way. General Electric, for example, offers to pay its suppliers electronically. Suppliers can continue with the traditional payments arrangement or shift to a new scheme in which payments are transferred electronically following delivery of the goods. Under the old method, cash flowed to suppliers sixty days or more after shipment. Under the new arrangement, payments can be virtually instantaneous. G.E. receives no discounts for prompt payment. The amount is the same regardless of method. As a supplier, which payment method would you prefer? New business methods like these will catch on very quickly.

The benefits to the supplier are significant, but why would the customer prefer rapid payment? The customer surrenders financial float, but receives considerable benefits in return. Once suppliers, producers, distributors, and customers are connected to an electronic payments network, orders can be placed electronically, reducing overhead and response time, and shrinking the purchasing department. The payables department can also be reduced. Ultimately, customers may be able to monitor suppliers' inventory positions, and production and delivery schedules, to fine-tune their orders and shrink their own inventories.

Stretch this logic to its ultimate conclusion and you find just-in-time payment. Payment on delivery provides a powerful incentive for suppliers to adopt just-in-time inventory management. Many firms already insist on just-in-time delivery from their suppliers, but still pay invoices on a traditional basis, thereby retarding a more complete shift to the new methods. In time that will undoubtedly change. Some supermarkets are beginning to pay suppliers only when an item is bought, not when it is delivered to the store. This pushes the logic even further, and ties suppliers ever closer to distributors.

If you can envision a different way of paying that frees up working capital, then you can also imagine many ways to put that money to work more creatively. Electronic funds transfer has been around for about a decade, but its impact on the way we conduct business still lies ahead.

Informationalized transactions also have lower variable costs. The cost of entering and processing an order in the average industrial business today ranges from $80 to $300 for even the smallest order. With electronic order entry and processing, variable costs shrink to almost nothing. That means smaller orders become more economical, reinforcing the trend toward just-in-time inventory management.

Imagine what impact informationalizing can have on the total economy. When the velocity of money rises sharply, it stimulates economic growth. Rapid response, just-in-time inventory, electronic payment, low overhead and working capital, all increase the velocity of money. The average firm carries 25 to 35 percent of its assets as working capital, rather viscous money that could be speeded up. There is over a trillion dollars in working capital in the United States economy. Shrink this as much as 75 percent by informationalizing, and vast resources are freed for more productive uses.

Firms that establish informationalized operations and relationships in any business will gain a significant edge because they provide much greater precision in ordering to exact specifications, shorter response times, working capital savings, and significant overhead reductions. As firms shift to these more powerful informationalized patterns of operation, the larger economy will begin to exhibit a very different profile. But this shift happens one firm, one relationship, one business at a time. This could mean a period of two decades before all firms, all relationships, and all businesses make the shift. During the process, those firms that build informationalized operations and relationships will thrive at the expense of those who wallow behind.

■ Informationalization + Direct Access = Higher Service Standards

Initially, those who resist new technologies bemoan the loss of the human touch but gradually make the switch as the manner of using them slowly blends into familiarity. With early telephones most calls were made through an operator. Customers picked up the phone and waited for the operator to say, "Number, please." No one, customer or company, wants to use an operator to place all calls today. Similarly, the ATM is replacing human tellers for bank transactions. The shift may take a decade or more, but it will occur. More and more transactions will be conducted without the aid of a human intermediary.

When we make hotel, airline, or car reservations today, we either call a travel agent or an 800 number. In both cases, we work through an intermediary who takes our request and enters the order—that is, after we have had the opportunity to listen to several minutes of telephone music and recorded voices. The next time you are put on hold, waiting to make an inquiry or reservation, remember, there's a better way. Smart vendors are now providing direct electronic query, decision support, order entry, and near-immediate delivery to the customer. Many customers would welcome services that allow them to scan options and enter orders directly, twenty-four hours a day. The customer is happier and a layer of overhead is removed.

Federal Express recently initiated a system that allows customers to enter parcel pickup requests directly into its master route schedule through a touch-tone telephone. They punch keys to specify their location code, number of packages, destination zip code, and pickup time. Federal Express is also developing electronic systems that will allow customers to access its shipment status data directly. Both services eliminate intermediaries who enter customer requests into corporate information systems. Citicorp's Citiline service allows customers with push-button phones to access their account balances, verify checks and deposits, and transfer funds without human assistance. In most cases, such as the choice between ATMs and bank tellers, parallel service options must coexist for some time, but the balance is shifting to direct customer access to services. Progress in the use of direct access methods is tied to their convenience and to educating and training customers.

Direct access means giving customers the ability to access all the vendor's products, services, and resources, and to configure any combination of them with seamless order entry, fulfillment, and settlement. It doesn't work that way today. Entering the 1990s, the more typical transaction is fragmented, inefficient, and frightfully painful to customers. That is even more true for industrial transactions, including the computer industry itself.

Imagine yourself in the Management Information Systems (MIS) department of a large corporation. You make a considerable effort, both for purchasing economies and planning purposes, to coordinate all purchase requests. Company-wide requests are collected, and a single consolidated purchase order is given to each vendor. One major vendor is a large computer company, for example, offering a full range of products and services. This month, your consolidated order calls for a set of personal computers, a minicomputer, software packages, a local area network package, data storage devices, the new version of the mainframe operating system, a high-end printer, a range of supplies, and a variety of services.

You present a single order to the vendor's sales representative, but this vendor is organized into twelve product divisions, each with its own order entry system, unique formats, and a different identification code for the same customer. Although that problem can be surmounted with cost and delay, the larger problem cannot. The customer wants the PCs and printer connected with the LAN and installed simultaneously. That also has to be coordinated with installation of the minicomputer, conversion of the mainframe operating system, and the provision of several other services. The customer also wants a single itemized bill but, again, this vendor has six different billing systems, each with different formats and codes. The customer now needs to add a staff layer to interpret invoices, and the vendor needs to add staff to respond to customer queries about billing details. This is why the computer revolution has not made demonstrable increases in productivity.

Some firms are pretty good at hiding their operating flaws from customers, while others make it painfully obvious. In this all-too-typical case, the customer cannot easily access the full set of resources the vendor has to offer, nor configure a desired combination of products and services. Staff overheads are required by both parties to manage the relationship. Response delays and the costs of order entry, processing, fulfillment, and payment are considerable. Firms doing business this way are doomed to fail as informationalized rivals provide customers with much higher levels of service.

Today, many banks are offering customers direct access to the full range of their services through a single vehicle. This allows customers to select from dozens of services, including checking and savings accounts, credit cards, mutual funds, brokerage services, CD's, automatic bill payment, funds sweeping and transfer, and a wide range of additional options. Customers may configure unique sets of financial services to their own specifications. What's more, they may control the format, frequency, and mode for reporting these services by themselves. Going into a traditional financial institution with a lengthy shopping list used to mean "bring your lunch and some Excedrin." During the next decade increasingly it will mean superior standards of customer service in more and more industries.

The spread of computerized reservations services throughout the airline industry has been swift and complete. In addition to speeding reservations and ticketing, travel agents utilize them to improve productivity dramatically, cut back-office overhead by eliminating paperwork, speed payments, shorten cycles, and sharply increase customer service. Would you work with a travel agent who books flights the old way, with multiple phone calls to verify all flight options, no advanced seat selection or boarding passes, and lengthy ticketing delays? Now, of course, we do not even need to work with a travel agent to secure these services. American Airlines' "Eaasy Sabre" service and OAG's flight reservations service are available directly to the customer through channels such as Dow Jones, Prodigy, and CompuServe. When customers shift to electronic distribution channels, traditional channels wither. That may happen to travel agents, and it certainly applies to retail operations in general.

■ Informationalization = Interorganizational Bonding

The American organizational model in the industrial economy held transactions in the open market at arm's length but encouraged intimate internal coordination, despite bureaucratic impediments. Organizational models in some countries, such as Japan, maintained linkages as intimate among companies as within them. The maturation of the information economy in the United States is drawing us closer to the fraternal model, and away from arm's-length transactions.

The distinction between internal and external transactions blurs, as customers directly set vendors' specifications, schedules, credit, terms, and settlement. Suppliers, distributors, and even retail consumers become closely intertwined with producers through sophisticated information architecture. Over the next two decades, these features will come to dominate the way all business is transacted in start-ups and corporate giants, high- and low-tech, manufacturing and services. The blurring of company boundaries will, in turn, create a host of new problems together with the greater opportunities.

Security and independence, for example, become major issues within the electronically linked companies and are reasons for firms to resist the trend. Managers often do not want to give customers and suppliers access to critical data and to their operating systems, and use the security issue as a cultural crutch to resist change. Concern with security is valid, but there are many ways to limit the problem, and it need not be a show-stopper. Authorization codes, verification procedures, transaction boundaries, and third-party escrow insurance services can address the issue.

Florida Power and Light, an electric utility with a notable record in the advanced use of information technology, has implemented an interesting solution to the security problem by placing its suppliers into five categories, according to their degree of electronic integration. The first tier includes traditional qualified suppliers, the second only those with EDI linkages. By the fifth tier, FP&L and suppliers have reciprocal direct access to virtually all of each others' information infrastructure, including data bases and operating systems. By mutual consent some suppliers stay in a certain category indefinitely. Additional benefits flow to each party as they increase their electronic integration, however, and this provides incentives to move to a closer linkage.

■ Informationalization + Logistics = Globalization

National and global competitors can approach the response times of a local service outlet by informationalizing operations that are located almost anywhere. Distance is disappearing as a limiting factor in all business operations. Thanks to sophisticated information and logistics linkages, businesses are relocating and reconfiguring their activities into global value-added chains, based on least cost and greatest expertise.

If you ever look at a circuit board, for example, you will find chips and components from a dozen or more countries. The manufacturers are coordinating a global network of suppliers. Even the custom chips that displace whole circuit boards utilize global production networks. VTI's chips are designed in one of the company's centers in North America, Asia, or Europe, or at a customer location anywhere in the world. The specifications are then transmitted to Silicon Valley where photo masks are produced. These are shipped to Japan where silicon wafers are etched. The completed wafers are shipped to Korea for dicing and mounting, and the chip assembly is completed in Malaysia. The final product is shipped directly to the customer, avoiding additional distribution links. None of this can be accomplished without information linkages and logistics partners, both critical infrastructure services that are taking shape rapidly.

Globalization is easiest for products with high value-to-weight ratios, like semiconductors, but with the aid of logistics partners it is occurring in all businesses. Federal Express, DHL, and UPS are battling to be those partners. Forty-eight-hour global service to heavy volume areas is becoming common. As the overnight delivery business matures, the next iteration of the industry's life cycle might be defined as the battle to become not just the distribution arm for corporate America, but the logistics arm for the global economy.

Printing has been a local business because of shipping costs. Technological developments enabled it to become a national business late in the industrial economy. Printing and communications technologies in the first half of this economy then made possible simultaneous local printings of national papers and magazines, such as the *Wall Street Journal* and *Time*. Now, information technologies are allowing the economies that are making printing a global business. Japanese catalogs and magazines, for example, are now commonly printed in Hong Kong and mailed directly to customers in Japan. Hong Kong exports more than $400 million in printing products each year. McGraw-Hill, *Newsweek*, and others use Hong Kong as part of global production networks. Singapore and then Korea are close behind as printing exporters.

Banks, credit card companies, and airlines use sites in the Caribbean for check and voucher processing. Ireland is a growing center for insurance policy and claim processing for U.S. insurance companies. Lexis, a computerized legal reference service in Dayton, Ohio, uses Korean keypunchers to enter legal documents, briefs, and abstracts into its computer system. In this and other cases, sacks of paper are shipped to data entry shops, stand-alone businesses located anywhere in the world, and completed electronic files are wired back to the customers.

Returning to our bathroom fixture example, American Standard's marketing executives anywhere can specify product features appropriate for local customers. The product designs are developed in Italy, and precise engineering specifications are done at the West German CAD/CAM unit and then transmitted to the master mold facility in France. Master molds are shipped for production to flexible manufacturing facilities in Germany, Korea, or Mexico. Each function is performed, independent of location, wherever the expertise and economies reside.

Whenever possible, the information component is stripped from the tangible product and moved around the world on sophisticated information systems like the ones we have described. The greater economic value generally resides in this no-matter information. Logistics partners enter at the points where the information must reconnect with solid product, what the mature business used to consider "the real stuff." Global production systems, linked by global communications and logistics systems, are appearing in virtually all manufacturing industries and in a growing array of service businesses.

■ Beyond Jack Benny and King Lear

The infrastructure for our economy has matured to the point where it is transforming the conduct of all enterprises. The internal efficiencies that it creates in the organization, and the external added service value that it provides in the marketplace, are the stuff by which older generation businesses are learning to enjoy life after forty.

Specifically, these include such trends as mass customized products that are made, delivered, and paid for in real time; the growing importance of distribution and delivery activities and their increasing absorption of manufacturing's role; the substantial shrinking of inventory, overheads, and working capital; direct electronic access by suppliers, producers, distributors, and consumers to the full resources of one another; the consequent blurring of boundaries among these entities; the likely evolution of electronically married groupings; and also the globalization of enterprise that comes from combining developments in communications and logistics. These trends are not independent of one another, but mutually reinforcing. Collectively they sketch an emerging model for how existing businesses will conduct their affairs.

Beyond the transformation of existing older businesses, however, and born from within them, all of these trends are also spawning an entire generation of new businesses. Not all businesses deny their advancing age like Jack Benny, or bemoan the loss of their once-great power like King Lear. With informationalizing, they still thrive. And many are starting to rejoice in the new generation of businesses that they are bringing forth.

CHAPTER 3

Find the Turbocharger in Your Business

Like leaves on trees the race of man is found,
Now green in youth, now withering on the ground;
Another race the following spring supplies:
They fall successive, and successive rise.

Homer, **The Iliad**, Book 6

The industrial economy produces and emits waste by-products. We call them pollutants or consider them useless, but some of these by-products can be, and have been, put to better use. Natural gas is a classic example. Originally burned off at the wellhead as worthless, it became a major industry when infrastructures and markets were developed. Turbochargers, another example, recycle engine exhaust fumes to greatly increase performance and power.

The information economy also produces information exhaust, and it too can be turbocharged. Information exhaust can be captured, processed, and recycled to improve business performance. Opportunities exist to provide *turbocharged information* services in all businesses and industries. In fact, a new generation of enterprises built around information emitted from older businesses is already taking shape. The irony is that *turbocharged information service businesses often become worth more than the businesses from which the information was generated in the first place.*

TV Guide, for example, was purchased in 1987 by empire builder Rupert Murdoch for more than $2 billion. This publication is essentially nothing more than a well-packaged listing of television broadcast schedules, information that is available to anyone from a number of sources. Despite this, the purchase price for *TV Guide* had a market valuation higher than any one of the major broadcast networks, CBS, ABC, or NBC, at that time. Why would a program list be more valuable than a broadcast network?

The *Official Airlines Guide* (*OAG*), a listing of monthly flight schedules, was sold in 1988 for $750 million. OAG simply consolidates flight information, yet this basic concept created a business with a greater market value than all but the largest airlines. At the time, its purchase price was about three times what TWA paid for Ozark Airlines, almost triple the value of the Eastern shuttle, and only slightly less than the market valuation of U.S. Air. Why would a list of flights be worth more than an airline?

Quotron provides information about security prices to brokerage companies. Purchased by Citicorp in 1986 for $628 million, Quotron did not possess proprietary access to securities information. It simply filled a need that brokers hadn't attended to, by capturing securities transaction information and recycling it back to the brokerage industry that generated the information in the first place. This created a business with a market value greater than the prices paid for several leading brokerage houses in the late 1980s, including Paine Webber and Smith Barney. Why would a company that simply lists price quotes be worth more than companies that evaluate those quotes and execute the actual buy/sell transactions, even when it does not make a profit?

The proper order of things seems to be standing on its head. It would appear that TV programs are produced and broadcast to create a need for *TV Guide*. During downturns in the airlines industry, there are times when it would seem as if someone has to fly airplanes so that money can be made selling flight information and reservation services. The brokerage industry's dismal performance in the late 1980s and early 1990s made the income from financial information services look sublime. Telerate, a principal provider of bond pricing data, was acquired in late 1989 at a valuation of over $2 billion. E. F. Hutton, the second largest brokerage concern in the United States, was sold at about the same time for less than $1 billion. Someone, it would seem, has to perform brokerage services so that profits can be made selling financial information services. If a telephone company makes more money from the Yellow Pages than from its standard telephone service, does that mean telephone service is provided so that the Yellow Pages can be published? Of course not. But information offshoots represent a tremendous business opportunity, and every business contains one or more latent info-businesses.

New offshoot businesses that start as simple activities in support of the main attraction will surpass core businesses in market value in many industries. Flying people back and forth, broadcasting TV programs, selling stocks and bonds, and a million and one other activities may become rather unpromising economic affairs if they are pursued in the traditional manner. We have seen how the mature businesses of the older generation can modernize themselves by informationalizing their internal operations and service to their customers. Here we will see how some of these support activities may become information-based businesses in their own right.

The opportunity to create value by providing information related to the primary product or service exists to some degree in all businesses. The ability to see and develop those opportunities, however, is realized by far fewer businesses, even though it is central to their future success. Not one of the television networks grasped the opportunity developed by *TV Guide*. The airlines missed the *Official Airlines Guide*, and brokerage houses missed the financial information services opportunity developed in Quotron. Citibank and Dow Jones, Quotron's and Telerate's respective owners, are still debating their strategic logic in making these acquisitions, and for making them profitable in the near term. Before this economy reaches its peak, many other traditional firms will watch independent entrepreneurs and more advanced competitors capture the richest prize within their market—collecting, processing, and selling critical information generated but unappreciated by the core business.

Who will capture this prize in your industry? It could be a progressive firm or two from within the older core businesses, as happened in the airlines with reservation systems. Or it may be one or two new entrants from outside the old power structure, such as the new players trying to restructure financial intermediation. Or it may be several companies working together in a cooperative association, such as we described in the apparel industry. In many industries, all of the above and more will be vying to define and dominate information pathways.

Firms that informationalize their core businesses stand a good chance of seeing and seizing info-business opportunities, but many will be grasped by new ventures. These new generation businesses, whether formed as an extension of an existing business or as a new venture, will add a new layer of services to the economy. The aggregate effect will be a turbocharged, high-performance economy. But it will happen one business at a time.

■ TRW Finds a Turbocharger

The new generation businesses are developing in industrial manufacturing firms as well as in entertainment, airlines, broadcasting, and other services. TRW, for example, is still thought of as an auto parts and aerospace company, with each of these businesses generating over $3 billion in annual sales. This giant of industrial manufacture and high-tech engineering, however, contains a thriving info-business that could eventually dominate the firm's growth and profits. The new generation business is housed in the company's Information Services Group (ISG), which represents less than 10 percent of total sales but accounts for almost 25 percent of TRW's total profit. The market value of its information service businesses certainly exceeds the value of its traditional businesses. TRW is growing new generation information businesses from within an older generation industrial company.

The Credit Services Division, ISG's main unit, operates a data base containing 145 million records of individual credit histories, including credit card, retail, leasing, mortgage lending, and other credit data. TRW provides credit ratings to financial institutions, retailers, employers, business associates, and many other buyers. It launched a "Credentials" service in 1988 to provide consumers access to their own data and to serve as a credit reference.

TRW's business development projects aim to integrate other sources of information into their current credit-base core, which is already the world's largest assembly of individual financial information. By integrating demographic, family, Social Security, medical, and other data with credit histories, TRW can greatly increase the value of its information resources and expand its range of both services and customers. This master data base, referred to as Big Mother, represents the ultimate asset in an information economy. Enhancement and extension of that data base are central thrusts of ISG's growth strategy.

But the master data base is only one facet of TRW's info-business development program. A series of other ventures has been launched. One of TRW's broad initiatives is in the real estate transaction services business. Almost every real estate deal in the country involves a long list of often tedious steps: a title search, title insurance, escrow and legal services, mortgage application, review, and issuance, property insurance, and other activities. As anyone who has bought a house knows, each of these steps can be costly and time-consuming.

At present, for example, it can take thirty days or more to complete a title search alone. TRW has begun to offer electronic title search services. By building title data bases from public information sources, it can validate titles and issue title insurance almost instantaneously. With its credit analysis skills, it has the potential to offer real-time mortgage application and review services. Such services enable Citicorp to make a mortgage commitment within fifteen minutes, and Canada Trust in Toronto to issue loans by phone. All this can be done only by informationalizing the mortgage lending business.

Other revenue opportunities exist in the real estate information services field. The title data base could be used to offer property tax billing and collection services to municipalities. Title data, cross-referenced with credit history, could be used to offer market research and market segmentation information. Knowing who has listed, sold, or purchased property would be invaluable to many businesses, and this information constitutes another significant revenue opportunity.

The TRW example begins with a data base, the core asset in any information business, and a network provides real-

time direct access to the information resources for intermediaries or principals. Some info-businesses will go beyond
providing information to execute transactions. You may be
able to both look up and purchase an airline seat or a theater
ticket, for example. At present, TRW focuses on providing
information support to financial institutions and agents who
complete real estate transactions. But ultimately, many of
these services could be provided directly to the principals,
and the service can grow beyond information support to the
actual execution of a transaction.

The largest opportunity of all in real estate might be in
the electronic brokerage business. Currently, real estate brokers earn a commission of 6 percent or more on the sale of
every listed property. The principal role of the broker is to
bring the buyer and seller together. The real estate broker,
like the freight forwarder or travel agent, could be displaced
or complemented by a comprehensive information service
that brings buyers and sellers together. Buyers might use
terminals to search through video clips of properties that
meet their size, price, and location criteria and then contact
the listing broker or the seller directly. Television stations
started offering related services in 1985, with half-hour
shows picturing houses for sale. But television realty today
offers only a fixed sequence of properties: tomorrow's service
will ask the potential buyer for criteria on neighborhood,
number of bedrooms and bathrooms, parking, square foot-
age, style, and price, among others. Only self-selected properties will be viewed and the video clips will be interactive,
allowing the buyer to control the video tour. Twenty properties, instead of only a few, can be reviewed in an hour. All
of this may merely pre-screen homes prior to personal visits
with a traditional broker, but don't be surprised if properties
begin to sell without physical tours, and perhaps even without brokers, especially to foreign investors. Such a service
would revolutionize the industry by eliminating cumbersome intermediaries and introducing new-age information
services that simplify and speed up the transaction process.
It could even lead to remote purchases of real estate prop-

erties and increasing investments by foreign buyers, particularly in countries with disadvantaged trade and currency positions.

■ The New Age "Infomediaries"

The intermediaries of the industrial economy, such as real estate agents, are often displaced, or their functions are transformed, when businesses are informationalized. Their demise is paralleled by the rise of new-age "infomediaries" such as TRW's Credit Services and Tele-realty services. Infomediaries are enterprises that use the various forms and functions of information to link buyers and sellers electronically.

Infomediaries can also link producers and consumers, those upstream and downstream, providers and users, and senders and receivers. They add value by enabling these parties to get better and quicker information from one another. With convenient and direct access twenty-four hours daily, they deliver real-time results to meet customer needs. Infomediaries are superior to traditional intermediaries that offer more expensive, time-consuming, and limited fare. They furnish a wider range of options than the traditional services do, because they consolidate information unavailable from any other single source. Rather than going through lengthy and multiple steps, they handle inquiries, processing, and transactions all at once. They facilitate customized transactions, and can preview outcomes of any selection or decision. Informationalized intermediaries or infomediaries will create and provide these services to participants in all businesses within a generation. Those businesses that do not informationalize within that time in all likelihood will be out of business.

Like the leaders of the businesses of the industrial economy who built their empires by laying railroad tracks and highways, the creators of the new infomediaries are building their empires on electronic tracks that will direct the movement of an industry's information. And now that the com-

puter and telecommunications infrastructure is being constructed, the race is on to establish dominance in the info-businesses. For the next fifteen or so years, the third quarter of this information economy, each major business sector will experience the proliferation of information channels, followed rapidly by a shakeout and finally the consolidation of a few leaders among these enterprises.

Fragmented channels will give way to one or two dominant infomediaries in each industry. These leaders will provide the primary electronic distribution pathways for the most profitable slices of business, the information services. The new infomediaries will ultimately represent the principal means of access for buyers and sellers in all businesses by the time the information economy matures, that is, before 2010. Participation in these electronic channels inevitably will become necessary, and virtually all firms will be represented on the dominant systems.

■ The New Generation of Financial Infomediaries

The shift to new infomediaries will perhaps have the greatest ramifications in financial services. The linkup between sellers and buyers is being transformed in all financial markets: especially in stocks, bonds, options, futures, and currencies, but also spreading to insurance, real estate, and other related financial services. The exchanges, with all the pandemonium, drama, and abuses of the trading pits, are the old intermediaries. Their very existence is being threatened by the new infomediaries who want to replace the exchanges with electronic trading, and establish new standards and networks. At stake is nothing less than the direction and control of the world's financial infrastructure.

The global bond market alone trades over $4 trillion daily, with millions changing hands electronically every second. Despite its size, however, there is no central exchange for trading bonds, and prices vary from one brokerage firm to another. The contest is on, therefore, to establish and direct a global electronic bond market. The first challenge is to get bond price data flowing instantaneously from all exchanges and transactions through a network to customers' screens. With that foot in the door, the second challenge is to get bids and offers coursing over the same network. Major contenders in this contest include the world's largest brokerage houses (Nomura, Daiwa, Merrill Lynch), commercial (Citicorp) and investment banks (First Boston, Salomon Brothers, Goldman Sachs), and publishers (Reuters, Dow Jones, Knight-Ridder), as well as a couple of daring entrepreneurs.

Six major banks formed a consortium in 1989, now called simply the "Electronic Joint Venture," to provide bond trading information services to themselves and others. The six— First Boston, Goldman Sachs, Morgan Stanley, Salomon Brothers, Shearson, and Citicorp—account for about 25 percent of all bond trading. That should give them a strong starting advantage in the race to capture the bond trading info-business. As is the case in most industries, however, independent outsiders appear to have a very good shot at the prize. Meet the main contenders.

Telerate Inc., now fully owned by Dow Jones & Co., dominates the electronic bond-info-business, serving 75,000 terminals. Telerate built a $500 million business, with a stock market valuation of over $2 billion, by acquiring real-time transaction data for government bond sales between the U.S. Treasury and the thirty-six primary security dealers. Those data provide critical real-time reference points for bond dealers and brokers, and serve as definitive market prices for transactions in other bond markets.

Reuters, sending news and financial information to over 200,000 terminals worldwide, is the largest and most aggressive participant in financial information services and electronic trading. Besides its news services, it has ventures in satellite communications, trading room screens, and data networks for foreign exchange and equity trading.

Bloomberg Financial Markets, 30 percent owned by Merrill Lynch, is a third important entry. The Bloomberg service offers highly sophisticated analytical capacity in addition to basic data. According to one customer, for example,

A bond's value can be altered by dozens of arcane factors, ranging from early redemptions to coupon-reinvestment rates to principal repayment rates. The Bloomberg can calculate what a bond would be worth if any of these factors change. It also compares the value of different securities and shows historical data. Rival machines offer less data and cruder calculations.

If we wanted to sell seven-year bonds and buy two- and ten-year bonds in their place, it could tell us if the trade was worthwhile in a minute.[1]

Paying homage to the system that started it all, Bloomberg wants to "sabre-ize" his terminals, that is, sell them to rivals and list the bond prices of all brokerage houses on the same screen. If bond sellers and buyers all over the world used one open system, bond trading would be revolutionized. Comparative price displays on a single screen would narrow the spreads between bid and asked prices, make arbitrage windfalls more difficult, and reduce the importance of analysts. Executing the transactions electronically would eliminate most traders, as happened at the London Stock Exchange in 1986, and it also holds the promise of lower costs, less price gouging, and global round-the-clock trading hours. Now, when the bond market in one city closes for the day, the buy and sell order books are passed on successively around the globe to markets in time-zones that are still open. The electronic market would never close.

That pattern has already appeared in the trading of foreign currencies. In contrast to other financial instruments, there is no physical foreign exchange market but a round-the-clock network of traders who communicate and execute billions of dollars in transactions electronically, over digital networks. Daily foreign exchange trading volume in London, New York, and Tokyo alone exceeded $600 billion in 1990, a fourfold increase in three years. The massive growth in foreign exchange trading could only occur because of sophisticated information infrastructures that have been deployed in recent years. In particular, the completion of high-speed fiber optic links between London, New York, and Tokyo allows real-time integration of the three major financial centers. Sophisticated information systems that utilize these data highways have been developed to permit electronic order entry, processing, fulfillment, and payment.

One such system is the Reuters Dealing service. Reuters has long been the principal source of foreign exchange information to currency traders, with over 200,000 terminals on traders' desks around the world. These terminals are connected to Reuters computers in London, New York, and Hong Kong by what may be the world's largest private communications network of leased lines and satellite dishes. But until 1981, Reuters was solely in the business of providing support information to traders. With the debut of its Dealing service in that year, its clients were able to execute currency transactions directly with one another over their terminals.

Reuters' 11,000 Dealing terminals generated well over a million transactions a month in 1990, and accounted for a third or more of all currency trades. But those trades are not centrally processed. They are an electronic version of a telephone trade between two parties. In December 1989, Reuters introduced its Dealing 2000 service. With this new service, clients can enter buy and sell orders directly into their terminals. These orders will be matched automatically and anonymously with others from around the world, executed and reported electronically by Reuters computers on Long Island, New York.

The new service will be tempting. Bond brokers charge commissions of about $100 per $10 million to both parties in any transaction. The Reuters service will charge a flat fee of $25, to the buyer only, regardless of the size of transactions. This new service will mean more trading volume, more liquidity, and a more efficient market, reinforcing the globalization and informationalization of financial markets, and all conducted over a private network.

While foreign exchange markets are most advanced, other financial markets are moving quickly in this same direction. Reuters again plays an important role in several. Its Instinet stock trading service, for example, operates an electronic trading network for institutional investors in U.S. and British securities. Daily trading volume averages more than ten million shares, still only a small fraction of trading volumes on the New York and London exchanges, but a growing factor in equity trading. Reuters also holds a stake in global electronic commodity trading. Together with the Chicago Mercantile Exchange, it recently launched the Globex computerized commodity futures trading service. This service is envisioned as a twenty-four-hour electronic trading vehicle for retail users worldwide.

Reuters is not the only player in the electronic trading arena. Quotron is moving beyond its traditional role as a source of security information to offer electronic securities trading services. Bloomberg Financial Services, also expanding beyond information support, has already established a sophisticated electronic bond trading service. Telerate is also in a position to enter this arena. Japanese banks now operate several powerful private bond, currency, and security-trading networks. These systems could easily be converted to public services.

Globex marks a critical step in the evolution of financial markets. All of the other services mentioned above are wholesale only, that is, they are accessible only to existing brokers and traders. It is as if a smart Tele-realty service could only be accessed through a traditional real estate agent's office. In many industries information services may be accessible only through traditional channels, but there are significant opportunities to extend these new services directly to individual consumers. Globex aims to bring the trading floor directly into your home, completely bypassing the traditional intermediaries as well as the old trading mechanisms.

For all of the apparent advantages of retail electronic trading, it still is not a business where one can say, "I have seen the future, and it works." The obstacles are enormous, and mainly involve market power and psychology, not technology. Unlike other industries, informationalizing the exchanges primarily affects the big money makers, not the hourly paid worker. Some businesses, like the Chicago Mercantile Exchange, feel that offering direct customer access to the trading "floor" is in their best interest, but most insist that the competitive edge comes from the touch and feel of the actual trading floor, not of the computer screen. Exchanges also provide liquidity, from traders willing to take the other side of any trade, that electronic trading will find hard to match.

The financial services industry stands at the forefront of informationalization. Its experience suggests that powerful conflicts between traditional intermediaries and new infomediaries can be expected. Traditional intermediaries want to control information resources and networks, and incorporate them into existing channels and customer relationships. New entrants, on the other hand, may give customers direct access to electronic markets. Thus, it is not just a question of which player will capture the information services channel, but how that channel will be defined. The two key dimensions are decision support versus execution and wholesale versus final customer accessibility. Wholesale infomediaries do not allow customers direct access to information services and electronic markets in a specific business. Infomediary retailers offer customers direct access to information and trading services.

The principal reason for a closed information services market is to reinforce an existing industry structure. Today, the primary foreign exchange market is a wholesale electronic market accessible to only selected institutions. If you or I want to buy foreign currencies, we will pay a large spread over the actual rate. If the official rate for British pounds is $1.90 per pound, we will pay $2 per pound when buying but receive only $1.80 when selling. The difference is the bank's or trader's margin. Their profits would shrink enormously if the public or corporate customers, who are often smaller financial institutions, achieved direct access to the electronic market and its superior rates. When only existing industry participants are allowed access to a central information network, they control both new competitive entries and customer access. Only registered real estate brokers, for example, can utilize the Multiple Listing Service. If anyone could enter a property for sale, or directly browse through listed properties, the broker's role as an intermediary would be diminished or eliminated.

The example of electronic securities trading shows that when a few large institutions account for a great percentage of total market activity, and for all of the high-volume transactions in a given business, they can create a highly efficient electronic market built on a private network, with high entry barriers. Other businesses and consumers will have to pay a fee to the gatekeepers who control access to the services.

■ Will Competition in the Future Be More Open or More Closed?

The new generation of infomediaries may not be any more open than was the old form of competition. In financial services, for example, they may provide us with more efficient means to conduct our monetary activities, but they may also strive to maintain limited direct access to electronic markets for both customers and competitors. They will determine how open or closed access will be for both buyers and sellers, and for both customers and providers. Real estate brokerage and foreign exchange trading demonstrate the restrictive end of the continuum, in that information and trading services are not directly accessible to the buyer or seller. In contrast, American's new "Eaasy Sabre" service, the retail reservation and ticketing service available over Compu-Serve, the Source, Prodigy, and other videotex networks, offers an open market from the retail side.

Many established firms will seek to restrict direct access to information and trading services. In the process, they may create competitors. Closed systems are a major reason for the growth of independent infomediaries. In contrast to traditional firms, they offer customers direct access to information resources and electronic transaction services. Independent services also appear because existing companies in many traditional industries are only interested in selling their own products and services. Value to the customer, nevertheless, is created by consolidating data from all participants. Few people want to know about the programs on only one broadcast channel or about the flights on only one airline. The stranded air traveler without access to an OAG or a travel agent would have to call several airlines before finding an acceptable flight and can never be certain of having the best option unless he or she calls all airlines.

The head of a major trucking company recently reacted to a proposal to develop an industry-wide trucking information service that matched shipping requests with trucking schedules. He said, "It's a good idea because it will improve utilization on back-hauls, reduce delays, lower fleet size, manpower, and energy costs, and overhead, and improve customer service. But we're not going to do this, because it would help the customer select competing carriers. Why would we do anything that helps sell our competitor's services?" The answer is, because it's a better business than trucking. *When existing industry participants neglect the information dimensions of their business, for whatever reasons, independent third parties emerge to fill this role.*

Third-party information clearinghouses bring together buyers and sellers in all sorts of businesses. FTD brings customers together with florists. Pizzanet is an infomediary that helps independent mom-and-pop pizza parlors compete against more informationalized home delivery pizza giants. Calls come into a central number and are farmed out to the nearest independent. The rest works like Domino's, the industry leader in pizza home delivery.

Creating a separable business based on the sale of industry-wide information services about all players, your competitors as well as yourself, is often a neglected opportunity. Independent third parties, not feeling constrained, oftentimes are better able to envision information services opportunities as separate stand-alone businesses. The *Journal of Commerce*, a Knight-Ridder, Inc., company, for example, offers a service to the shipping industry called Trans/ Rates which lists all schedules and rates for shipping companies in and out of the United States. Customers use this service to identify and select possible carriers based on convenience and cost. Without such a service, they would have to call several shipping companies or employ an intermediary, at some cost and delay, to identify options. Trans/ Rates is a valuable information service that might have been exploited by one of the major shipping lines, but wasn't. Why did an outside party capture this business? Possibly because each shipping company could not envision a service that might result in aiding customers to select another carrier. That posture, though understandable, neglects potential profit opportunities that may exceed returns in the primary business.

The emergence of such services depends, to some extent, on the willingness of competing companies to release information to the service provider. In the case of the shipping industry, the information is secured from the U.S. Maritime Commission, which requires all shipping companies to register their schedules and rates. No such examples yet exist, however, in hotel, trucking, insurance, and other businesses.

Hotel reservations today are organized around individual chains, yet a consolidated list would provide a superior range of options to the customer. The trucking industry in the United States also exhibits great opportunity for a comprehensive information system. Today, a customer needs to call a number of trucking companies or a broker to identify options. A comprehensive information service that listed all carriers and their rates and availability would be of great value to the customer and very profitable to the provider. Other infomediary businesses might be built by third parties around bringing together competing companies' insurance rates, limousine services, medical services, vacation travel packages, and many other businesses.

■ Cows, Cars, Crops, and Coins

Other opportunities for building infomediary businesses in electronic marketplaces have been anticipated for a number of years. Most have no particular focus on controlling the shape of an entire industry. They are, however, based on the same informationalizing principles we have been describing, and they include such mundane activities as selling cows, cars, coins, crops, haircuts, jobs, and junk.

Cows Cattle were sold in stockyards in the industrial economy, but video auctions on an electronic network could mean that stockyards would go the way of the old-fashioned cattle drive. Superior Livestock Auction, of Fort Worth, uses satellite transmission, television cameras, and computerized buying networks to auction steers that never leave the ranch until they are sold. This saves the time and cost of trucking, and eliminates the risk of injury and disease. By turning local cattle markets into a national and even international marketplace, the cattle also bring a higher price. More than a million cattle were sold over this network in 1990.

Cars Used cars are also being bought and sold over an electronic market. Car dealers often take trade-ins to make new car sales and periodically unload them in bundles to used car wholesalers, where they are redistributed through weekly auctions. The distribution system is regional, episodic, and cumbersome. The logistics requirements for physical movement of the cars are complex and costly. Today, electronic used car auctions are being held quarterly. Images and information about specific cars are transmitted over terminals to wholesalers who place bids electronically. Electronic auctions eliminate personal travel to auction sites and expand the market of buyers and sellers. If used cars can be sold electronically, anything can.

Crops Roger Brodersen, chief operating officer of Scoular Company, a major grain elevator and brokerage company, decided in 1983 that his company could profit by selling its internal information resources to farmers. He created an internal venture to transmit commodity prices directly to farmers. In 1986, Scoular sold the business to Brodersen for $900,000. His company, Data Transmission Network, now sends spot grain prices, futures quotes, and weather and other farm information to over 50,000 customers and has a stock market valuation in excess of $100 million.

Coins The rare coin market is a classic fragmented market of individual traders, brokers, and auction houses. Monthly price sheets or books give some reference points on coin values, but the coin market is highly idiosyncratic and inefficient. That is changing rapidly with the introduction of coin grading standards and coin pricing information. ANE ("Annie"), or the American Numismatic Exchange, now provides real-time price information on coin transactions by grade of coin over terminals. The next generation services will bring high-quality coin images and electronic trading to this market. And as this market has become more organized and efficient, major investment firms are now committing funds to coin investments. Merrill Lynch, Shearson, and other brokerage houses announced or launched coin investment limited partnerships for the first time in 1989. Funds from these new partnerships could double the demand for rare coins.

Haircuts Police artists who sketch descriptions of criminals now are aided by software that instantly adjusts their sketch according to the witness's commentary. TV audiences have been entertained with a similar piece of software that instantly changes any part of a person's face on a photograph. Want to see, for example, what President Bush would look like with Vice President Quayle's hair or eyes? Or Groucho Marx without the eyebrows? Presto! Watch the transformation occur on screen, before your own eyes. It's almost like hearing Robin Williams doing Hamlet as John Wayne, then as Jerry Lewis, and then as Bette Midler. Now imagine offering this software as a customer service in beauty parlors. A patron could see, before the fact, what the perm or rinse will look like. People could "try on" a variety of haircuts on screen before the scissors ever touch their hair. Cutting hair would become less risky, and the largest part of the economic value of the hairstylist could reside in the previewed information product. The same potential exists in a host of other businesses, including plastic surgery, landscape design, and interior decorating.

Jobs There is a need in the business world to bring together job openings and job seekers. Headhunters, or executive search consultants, serve as agents and intermediaries in this market. Because of the cost, delays, and ineffectiveness of such services, some companies have taken steps to create their own internal job market. Sun Microsystems, for example, receives thousands of job applications weekly. Sifting through them, matching them with job openings, getting the information into the right unit's hands, and so on, is an enormous task. Resumix, a software company, developed a program that reads and enters all applications into a standard format. This creates a data base that Sun then searches according to its staffing needs. A preliminary list of candidates and their records are sent via electronic mail to the department in need. The possibilities are screened and an E-mail message sent back to Personnel to set up job interviews with the appropriate few. All of this can now be done in minutes, not days.

Recruiters and headhunters came into existence to fulfill this kind of need, but they do so in a fragmentary way. Systems like Sun's are already in use within many headhunter firms, but all of them are treated as internal efficiency techniques, ways to improve the administrative performance of the organization. Perhaps some of them will be repositioned as open infomediary services, redefining the company's future business and replacing current inefficient and idiosyncratic job placement services.

Junk Yes, even junkyards are becoming electronic. Say, for example, that you wanted four 1976 Buick hubcaps. Our image of yesterday's junkyard has a greasy fellow kicking around in chaotic piles of old bent metal and muttering, "We might have one around here somewhere." Today, those greasy fingers punch in the item on a PC keyboard, and the electronic market searches instantly through all junkyards on the network. "Would you like those shipped UPS or regular mail, and how would you like to pay for your hubcaps, sir?" Like the informationalized haircut, the electronic marketplace greatly expands the junkyard's product inventory and its market boundaries, and the greater part of the value added in each transaction comes from the ability to locate the products, not from the products themselves.

■ You Can Informationalize Virtually Any Business

When any relatively standard product becomes an electronic blip on a computer screen, the fact that the blip represents a cow or a car becomes virtually irrelevant for the purpose of a transaction. When the bank held our home mortgage in yesterday's economy, it literally stored the document in its vault. Today's mortgages are written so that they can be packaged and sold as securities. Mortgage blips are now commodities, trading units to be bought and sold over and over in *secondary markets* where they are hedged, optioned, securitized, and cleared. Economist Robert Kuttner points out that while the ultimate in deregulation occurs in Third World bazaars, where every price is negotiable, consumers in advanced countries rely on posted prices. *With custom products and open electronic markets, prices also become customized.* But the possibility of gouging disappears as electronic markets expand the scope of offerings and vendors.

Computer systems have introduced periodic airfare adjustments, and the electronic marketplace is pushing us toward *continually adjusted pricing.* Imagine gas pump prices electronically linked to world oil prices. Or available airplane seats and theater tickets whose prices drop in order to clear the perishable inventory as the scheduled times draw near.

In vacation travel, a potentially large market exists in finding last-minute buyers for unsold and canceled vacation packages. Sellers list last-minute opportunities that are about to go to waste, and vacation buyers who are willing to go on short notice wherever the bargains are can scoop up huge savings. Last Minute Travel, of Alston Massachusetts, specializes in such Caribbean and Mexican vacations for New Englanders. Club membership is $35 a family per year, which includes a twenty-four-hour hot line with updated daily specials for the next fourteen days. One week in Jamaica, for example, might cost a Bostonian $300 for airfare and hotel.

There are probably similar opportunities to develop a secondary market in returned and rush concert, theater, and sports tickets in large cities. Since the value of the original product is about to evaporate, the added value of the infomediary may well be worth more than the item sold. Data banks for vacation condo time-shares use the same principle. This kind of electronic marketplace could create computerized trading of tickets, rental cars, and hotel rooms. Secondary and futures markets are likely to develop for a wide array of products and services.

The information economy is creating scores of niches within niches, or micromarkets. Videotex, for example, is a primary source of micromarkets. Videotex has a long and checkered history, but over the next decade it has a good probability of emerging as a central source of information services. It is evolving the most rapidly in France, where the Minitel system offers more than 13,000 different information services to over five million subscribers. Rather than building around home computers, these services are accessed through a video terminal that is connected to the telephone network. Terminals are installed free, with a target of reaching all French homes that have telephones by 1995.

Minitel permits the customer to access, process, store, and transmit a wide variety of information. As the videotex name implies, the Minitel network offers only minimal data processing, no sound, and almost no integration of the four forms of information. Nonetheless, it is the most successful and important precursor of future consumer networks in existence today.

The true power of these networks lies in the near-infinite wealth of information services that will be accessible to anyone. Electronic markets, for example, will permit buyers and sellers from around the world to list their wares and needs, to browse through offerings and requests, to compare prices, and to execute transactions, all electronically. Electronic markets will appear for every imaginable item from baseball cards to classic cars, pets, personal services, semiconductor chips, airplanes, and businesses themselves.

Remember, between now and 2005 the information infrastructure will be completed, and virtually everyone will be connected. Between now and 2020, literally tens of thousands of specialty markets may appear. Videotex provides electronic malls for entrepreneurs to set up shop alongside giant retail chains. Those who do well will offer many traditional benefits, such as convenience, lower cost, and more choice. They will also offer 2020 features, such as faster response, ease of use, more processing capability, mass customizing, and previewing of future outcomes.

Videotex services are essentially open networks. Anyone with access to the public telephone network and basic terminal equipment can participate in open electronic markets and information services. The electronic Yellow Pages is a currently developing example. Any vendor can be listed in the printed version of the Yellow Pages for a fee, and anyone can contact any listed vendor directly. The electronic version allows the public to evaluate vendors in greater detail by asking for price lists, menus, inventory in stock, and S&P ratings. Consumers can also conduct transactions: "Yes, I'd like to order six pairs of yellow cashmere socks, size eight." Imagine, for example, a service that lists all live entertainment options by city and state and offers ticket selection and sales services. That is simply an electronic extension of Ticketron, but now imagine a service that allows open access to both buyers and sellers. This service would provide a purchase verification code to the buyer and seller of the tickets and specify ticket exchange procedures. Open electronic markets of this sort will appear in all consumer businesses.

Think of open electronic markets as two-way classified ads. Anyone can list items for sale in the want ads, and anyone can contact a seller directly. Electronic want ads extend the function of classifieds even further through query and matching services and by providing broader geographic coverage if desired.

One of the problems with open networks is monitoring the integrity of buyers and sellers. As a case in point, just before Franklin National Bank went bankrupt in the late 1970s, it purchased a large quantity of foreign currency from Chase Manhattan. The foreign currency was transferred to Franklin, and went with it into bankruptcy proceedings. Franklin's debt to its trading partner also went into the bankruptcy court, resulting in a significant loss for Chase.

In electronic markets, particularly those involving significant funds transfers, the integrity of the participants is critical. One response is to limit participation to selected organizations or individuals who have been prescreened to ensure integrity of transactions. That is part of the logic for closed networks. The open market mechanism may be unable to guarantee such integrity, but there are means of structuring activity to minimize fraud. Sellers can be reassured by immediate funds transfer. Buyers face the same risks faced in any want ads transaction, but they may be compounded by the lack of personal contact or physical inspection of the product.

In anonymous transactions involving two unknown parties in a non-recurring purchase, the risks of fraud, deception, or simple misunderstanding are significant. There are, however, ways to manage these risks. Market makers can add value by offering escrow services, insurance, seller and buyer "credit" ratings, bonded warehouses, video inspection, and other features that address the needs of their customers. Solutions can be found to minimize the issue of transaction integrity.

■ Embedding Intelligence in Your Products

Besides providing information services to corporations and consumers through either open or closed infomediaries, a third alternative exists. In some instances it makes the choice between open and closed routes irrelevant. This alternative is *"embedded intelligence."* Infomediaries store vital information centrally and make it available to customers over a network. Continuing breakthroughs in microelectronic technologies, however, increasingly mean that *information services can be embedded in a product and located on the customers' desktops or night tables.*

This is analogous to the debate that occurred in the mid-1970s to mid-1980s about central versus distributed processing. The dispute was where to locate the intelligence, or computing power—in a central computer and then download it to individuals over a network or locally in the machine at the customers' fingertips. As prices went down and memory and performance went up, the distributed, or de-centralized, approach clearly won.

Similarly, we can expect many new info-businesses to locate their information literally at the customers' fingertips: inside their telephones, televisions, computers, cars, and other products. Both consumer and industrial products of the industrial generation become new-generation smart products when information features and functions are embedded directly in them. Then toilets, cameras, and so on, become smart toilets, smart cameras, and smart so ons. Smart products and stand-alone information services can be complementary, but they are also potential competitors.

Elevators are an example where embedded intelligence and infomediary services complement each other. Elevators are a mature business and little money is made off the box itself. Otis Elevator Company created Otis-Line Service so that if anything starts to go wrong in one of its boxes, it is diagnosed and, if possible, self-corrected, within the box. Otherwise, a message is sent to the servicing office about what parts, labor, and maintenance are needed. The building owner is covered by the service contract, where the real profit lies. The bulk of the intelligence and service delivery is contained inside the box. Similar patterns are appearing in PBXs, which are stand-alone substitutes for the public telephone network, and in programmable controllers which can manage a wide range of automated activities on a stand-alone basis.

All businesses will witness the growth of new electronic distribution channels, or infomediaries. Traditional distributors may remain, but ultimately all distribution channels will be informationalized. Traditional intermediaries can continue as dominant entities only by informationalizing their activities and services. The transformed distributor becomes the equivalent of a closed infomediary service. You have, in effect, a "smart" travel agent, a "smart" real estate agent, or a "smart" securities broker.

This means that *while all businesses will informationalize, they will have the strategic choice to do so by embedding intel-*

ligence in their products and services and/or in their distribu-tion channels. They will also have to choose whether to do only one, one before the other, or both at the same time. Ultimately, all traditional products, services, and channels will be displaced or transformed. That is, however, a process that will take decades. Here are some predictions about the pace of transition.

Networks can now be used to access remote libraries, but how about having an electronic library *in* your own home? Encyclopaedia Britannica recently announced an electronic home encyclopedia. The entire 1990 edition is stored on op-tical storage discs accessed by typing requests onto a special home terminal or appropriate PC. The service provides topic search assistance, cross-references, interactive graphics, and permits updating of the discs. There is no conceivable limit to the range of information that could be made available in this form.

Digital Equipment Corporation's entire software library, for example, can be put on one CD-ROM (a compact disc that can be read but not written on) and installed together with a CD-ROM reader inside every box they sell. CD-ROM elim-inates the need for magnetic tapes, reams of paper documen-tation, and the like. Sister Software has its entire repertoire on hand. Entire service libraries would be available on de-mand, on-site rather than through a network. This technol-ogy allows DEC to embed all of its software in a physical product on the customers' premises. Then, DEC can charge for usage the way the gas company does, by taking a remote meter reading. Customers have convenient access to the full range of DEC software, but only pay for what they use.

In this vision, which is an entirely new marketing strat-egy for computer companies, it is what is on the CD-ROM and its usage that are their new-generation businesses. Now it is the computer company that would become the info-mediary, taking a fee for distribution the way regional telephone companies do for 900 numbers. Customers are charged for two things: initial access to the intellectual prop-erty and a service charge for usage. This technology also allows very customized pricing. The menu that comes up on the boss's and secretary's screen, for example, can be customized and charged differently. Each person using his or her own box decides on the particulars, what to use and what features it should have.

Here is an important message for the box builders: put a meter and a modem into every box you build. Whether it's a high-definition television or a desktop computer, if it can connect simply with infomediaries and the provider has a built-in billing mechanism—wow! There is no end to the customer services that can be offered. In fact, we'd recommend that the meter and modem be a giveaway, built into the box but not into the price. They would be loss leaders, necessary to establish the traffic. Again, the real profits lie in the traffic flowing through the boxes, not in the boxes.

Similar capability could be built into home electronic devices. Daily, weekly, or monthly electronic classifieds and catalogs could be electronically shipped directly to customers' homes and offices. If the box is a home TV, the same logic can be applied to send a movie that has been ordered from a central movie file. In each case, the technology used will ultimately transform the mind-set about what business you are in.

Selling info-accessories will also be a major opportunity in the years ahead. Accessories that allow basic products to expand their information dimension will be available for almost all products. We can already buy devices that automatically manage our lights and sprinklers, start our cars, and infomate our checkbooks. Cameras will not just capture images to generate pictures, but they will also take on other information functions. Polaroid internalized the processing function. Why shouldn't cameras also provide image editing, storage, retrieval, and transmission capabilities?

Cameras, telephones, televisions, recorders, ovens, toilets, and an endless number of consumer products can and will utilize the various forms and functions of information. Similar capabilities could be built into home electronic devices. Entire libraries of games, services, data bases, and programs could be pre-located in the home and delivered on demand with payment based on usage. These are not mere enhancements of existing products. By embedding information services in products, the "older generation" of businesses is informationalizing and transforming what they offer to customers. At the same time, they are dramatically changing where and how they sell. By linking their products to a "younger generation" of infomediaries, they create fundamentally new forms and functions, and hence new market opportunities.

■ An 80-20 Rule for the 2020s

These developments are likely to occur in the maturing quarter of the information economy. What will company profiles look like by the time we enter the final, aging quarter of this economy? What will be their probable revenue and profit mixes between their traditional and informationalized businesses? What will be the market value of each? By 2010 many, if not most, companies will have so blended these old and new businesses that the distinction will be more analytical than real. But peering at the future from midway through this economy, we see a profound change. The average firm will shift its focus from industrial-age products, services, and channels to new info-business lines and distribution channels. The new info-businesses will include services that provide turbocharged information, industry-wide product offerings, preview, twenty-four-hour access, and self-design features, and many of these services can become stand-alone businesses in their own right.

When we distinguish between core businesses of the old generation and informationalized service businesses now, new-generation lines rarely account for more than 25 percent of revenues or profits. The 80-20 rule in business states that 80 percent of your business comes from 20 percent of your customers. It takes the remaining majority of customers, and a large organizational overhead, to contribute the residual 20 percent. An information-age variant of this rule would be that by 2020, 80 percent of business profits and market values will come from that part of the enterprise that is built around info-businesses. Mature noninformationalized businesses, and again large organizational overhead, will account for 20 percent or less (see Figure 3.1).

	Revenue	Profit	Market Value
Predicted Shift in Business Patterns 1990 → 2010			
The Old-Generation Core Businesses	80% → 50%	50% → 20%	80% → 20%
The New-Generation Info-Businesses	20% → 50%	50% → 80%	20% → 80%

Figure 3.1

If the greater economic value is in the secondary, information dimensions of the businesses, why not shift resources and management attention to those activities? Just such a process began during the past decade. A few farsighted people in a few large corporations crafted such visions. They were going to create the megacorporations of the future, synthesizing a revitalized core business and a bevy of new-generation, information-based service businesses. The colossus providing one-stop shopping for all financial services, the combined plane-hotel-car rental-travel company, the advertising-consulting-accounting urge to merge, and the integrated communications leviathan—are all examples of visions that have foundered.

The dreamers always rush to put the vision into place, through merger and acquisition, within a couple of years. Few survive. In the rubble and aftermath, there lingers the sense that maybe such visions will come to pass in the distant future. But for now, the better part of wisdom, perhaps, refocuses on the core business, buttressing it with the internal growth of related information businesses. Many of these are still embryonic; a few are growing rapidly. In the long run, those that succeed may ultimately supplant the core. But until we close out the millennium, they will be seen and treated as support players whose major job is to insulate the corporation when the next down cycle hits again.

Two or three decades from now, however, turbocharged information activities will become the primary businesses, while what used to be primary may even be sold. But in the decade of the 1990s, we are likely to have balance more than succession. The technology, infrastructure, and market are not yet prepared for much more. The business cores in today's economy are like parents in their forties and fifties with offspring who are young adults. Twenty years from now, the older generation will start retiring and the younger generation will come into its own. But that is for the 2010s, the last quarter of the economy, not the third quarter we are about to enter.

The new generation of businesses won't overwhelm us as revenue producers in the short term, but they are fine profit makers, and Wall Street analysts already assign them a disproportionate share of companies' breakup value. These businesses have evolved from cost-saving efficiency moves to value-added services to customers and then to tiny business lines that keep on growing. They are the turbochargers, not the main engines, and although their returns can be extraordinary, in their early growth years they are still infants, big enough to survive but too small to be at the center of management's vision for the future.

When they reach around 30 percent of the total corporate profits, however, their quantitative heft will produce a qualitative transformation. By that time, the savvy players will know this trend will continue and accelerate. They will no longer be simply turbochargers. They will be generating their own power, and as management focus shifts to these new businesses, new principles and perspectives will move to center stage in the corporate mind. That will signal a profound transformation not only in the way an organization views the business world, but also in how it views itself.

CHAPTER 4

Is It Time
to Kill Your Organization,
Before It Kills Your Business?

---

*Every act of creation is first of all an act
of destruction.*

Picasso

Do you and your company spend less than two-thirds of your time and energies on your business, and more than one-third on your organization? If so, then you have a business that exists to support an organization, not an organization that exists to support a business. It may be time to kill your organization before it kills your business.

Just keep your ears open the next time you are in your office. Are all the people you meet, whatever their jobs, energizing about the business or about the organization? Are they thinking more about customers or employees? About competitors in the marketplace or competitors in the hallways? About products or protocol?

Remember, business and organization are not the same thing. A *business* applies resources to create products and services that meet market needs, in relation to competitors. Automobile, book, computer, defense, energy, and food companies are each in different businesses. An *organization* is the way in which those resources are administered—the housekeeping—which includes the structure, systems, employees, and culture of the organization. Constant awareness of this simple distinction between business and organization, so often forgotten or ignored, is the key to good management. When people keep it in the forefront of their minds, they stay focused on *why* they are keeping house, not the *way* they are keeping house. When they invert that order, they and their company lose their effectiveness. Good housekeeping should never be an end in itself.

■ Focus on Your Business More, and on Your Organization Less

If you work in a company, whatever its characteristics, the chances are good that you would like to have a more flexible organization. And a more innovative one. A more risk-taking and entrepreneurial organization, and one that is more creative, adaptive, and responsive to change. You want all those good things. But do you know what you'll have if you really get them? You'll have *more* organization!

If you *really* want all these marvelous attributes in your organization, the way to get them is to focus on your business more, and on your organization less. Today, poised halfway through our economy, there is too much talk about organization, producing too few results. The more it is discussed, the more we foster its runaway growth. The more managers focus on it, the more of it we will have. We need less organization, not more. Of course, we do need management and organization, but how do we get the kind that accurately suits our human and economic needs? Here's how you might begin.

The present organization is generally a poor predictor of the kind that is needed for the future and, therefore, of the kinds of changes that will have to be made. Since you should organize in relation to the kind of business you will be in, that not-yet-existing business is the best source of information for what the future organization should look like. The process is straightforward. First, get the best possible fix on the business you will become. Next, as best you can, understand what kind of organization it will take to run that future business. Then, compare the future organization with the one you have now, and initiate a plan to get you from here to there.

The best place to look for the basis of organization change is in the future business, and the worst place to look is in the current organization. The present organization, however, may be a good predictor of what will *prevent* you from developing the kind of organization you will need. Like all creatures, it has a vested interest in continuing to exist. Try telling a parent that the children are grown and no longer need parenting, or a business function or government branch that it is too powerful and needs trimming. Rather than correcting what is negative in your current organization, focus on trying to understand what kind of future business would be the most effective, and let the new organization evolve from it.

Arthur Andersen & Company, the big accounting firm, is attempting to do exactly that with their more-than-mature auditing business. Although Andersen leads the industry by far in snaring new public audit clients, there is not much growth there. The effort and pricing are difficult, and the risks of being sued for bad audits have spiraled. In search of growth, Andersen has built the world's largest information and technology consulting business, a unit that now represents 42 percent of its revenues. As might have been expected, the consultants complained first that they were being underrepresented in the power and reward structure of the organization. Then, as that balance shifted to reflect the shift in business mix, people in the traditional accounting culture inevitably began to worry that they were becoming relics.

What Andersen could have interpreted as an organization problem—low morale and loss of power and rewards by the dominant culture—they properly understood instead as the need to create new business opportunities. One of these includes the attempt to create "real-time audits," so that investors would have instant access to financial data. Andersen is also stressing a Specialty Consulting Group, which grew 45 percent to $140 million in fiscal 1989 and might contribute $500 million within four years. Here, for example, the company takes on tedious search procedures and related litigation and compliance services that clients would rather have someone else do.

Andersen's most audacious step, however, is to reinvent the accountant. Independent audits mean that accountants are at arm's length, outside the clients' firms. Andersen is testing its willingness to forgo this once-core business and supersede it with specialty financial contract management. If the company succeeds as it did with technical consulting, the accounting business will never be the same. Now a company can rent its chief financial officer from Arthur Andersen. The outsider becomes the ultimate insider! Treasury, business planning, relations with lenders and investors, and all the other sensitive financial functions are entrusted to the emissary.

Andersen will have to handle with utmost care the delicate issues that the move to insider raises both with clients and the accounting profession. Client company employees, for example, overnight will find themselves employees of Andersen. This redefinition from outsider to insider, however, will create more questions of organization in and about the client's company than in Andersen's own. But then, of course, Andersen can always sell clients more consulting services to address that problem. *It is better to solve your organization problems by creating business opportunities than by focusing on the organization per se.*

■ Why It Is Not *Yet* Our Job to Create New Models of Organization

Early in the century, the great economist Joseph Schumpeter said the key to understanding our business economy is that it "incessantly revolutionizes the economic structure *from within*, incessantly destroying the old one, incessantly creating a new one. This process of Creative Destruction is the essential fact about capitalism."[1] When economic structures tire out, they produce their own successors. Revolutionaries have sometimes used this thinking to justify very violent actions, although economic change need not be accomplished this way. As recent events in Eastern Europe have shown, some socialist regimes are working peacefully to destroy their old economies creatively.

In today's businesses, if we simply refine our methods of organization, we may ignore the rediscovery of a basic principle: Form follows function. The architects of the Bauhaus School of the 1920s (Breuer, Gropius, Mies van der Rohe), for example, reacting to overly ornate design, created an unornamented style in architecture. It marched under the minimalist banner of "functionalism." We, too, need to strip away refinements and ornamentations of our organizations, and let the form of the organization follow the function of the business.

Change specialists in the 1970s, like Dick Beckhardt at MIT, advocated this approach. As was appropriate to that time, they told us to get unstuck. Our first job, they maintained, was to "unfreeze" the current organization before we could create the new one. Their three-step process was unfreeze, change, refreeze. These steps made sense, and within the microcosm of a single company, managers expected to achieve a complete cycle of organization change in only a few years. That has proved to be too short a cycle for this economy. If this is a seven-decade economy, comprising the mid-1950s to the mid-2020s, the unfreezing, changing, and refreezing steps will each probably take a quarter century. In fact, we are far from finished unfreezing our organizations. Today's leaders, in their forties, fifties, and sixties, will be retired before we have created the great models for managing and organizing in the information age. Those models will come along only when the information economy itself has matured. And that is a generation from now.

In the decade of the 1990s, it is not our job just yet to create new housekeeping models. Rather, our job is to unfreeze current ways of looking at organization, to prepare the terrain and loosen it up for organizational change, so that when the new seeds appear they can be planted in fertile ground.

■ Creating a Real-Time Organization

Current organization models are not time-based. They still operate in a three-dimensional universe of being rather than becoming. This is another reason why it would be difficult to create, or even postulate, a future organization today.

Science and technology made time intrinsic to their models of how things work, and recently business has caught on to this newly perceived reality. Management Information Systems (MIS) and Strategic Planning, for example, are two functions that did not exist in corporations at the beginning of this economy. Today, they are present in virtually all companies and generally report directly to the top. They are functions that have made time intrinsic to their housekeeping ways. They focus on process rather than state. MIS taught us about "real time" and Strategic Planning has made us familiar with product life cycle and business life cycle concepts. Nevertheless, notions of a *real-time business* and of an *organization life cycle* are not widely held or used.

It would be a major advance in our housekeeping if we became aware that organizations, too, have life cycles—the life cycle clock also ticks for them. Let's examine what the life cycle stages look like for organizations, and how life cycles do or do not match, for economies, companies, and individuals, and for a business and its organization.[2]

If you think of organizations along a past-present-future time line, most lag behind the present reality. They are almost always trying to catch up and change because their managers sense that they are not quite right the way they are. Anyone who works in a large organization knows that this is not an easy task. By the time the change is implemented, the once-present is now again past, and the lag is still there. As yet, there is no such thing as a real-time organization, one that adjusts to match present-day business conditions continuously and instantaneously.

Deal-oriented businesses like investment banking are organized around rapid response as a basic housekeeping requirement, but exceptions such as these are not likely to provide a model that can be used by all businesses. A leading commercial bank, however, is trying a novel approach. Before completing a new headquarters building, the president stunned senior executives by telling them that no one would be assigned specific office space, secretaries, or other support personnel. Instead, each would have access to all the information, office facilities, and people needed to complete a particular task. The initial reception was not enthusiastic, and the results are not yet clear.

The actual implementing of a real-time organization will be an enormous task, first requiring additional development of the information infrastructure and information businesses. The step that can be taken now, however, is to factor time into our housekeeping framework. This is a mental shift and need not wait for technology. When we make it and treat our organizations within a time framework, then, we will explicitly differentiate their beginning, end, all the phases in between, and the patterned flow from one phase to the next.

Epigenesis is a biological phenomenon that has been very important for understanding this patterned flow in all life cycles. It has been usefully applied to individual psychology and has bearing as well on corporate psychology. Epigenesis holds that embryos are created entirely new and develop in a determined way. The lenses of the eyes, for example, are supposed to appear in the seventh week of gestation, but if they don't, they are not going to pop up in the seventeenth week. The message, equally appropriate for companies, is that if things don't develop at their appropriate time, they are not going to develop at a later one.

Erik Erikson, the noted psychologist, used this notion to spell out the various phases of a person's life cycle. Each stage of life, according to Erikson, is characterized by a central task. If the task is successfully negotiated, a person moves on to the next phase of life more complete and fulfilled. If not, the person moves on to subsequent stages of life but always remains troubled by the issue that he or she failed to come to terms with at the appropriate time. Basic trust, for example, must be mastered in infancy; it cannot be put off until childhood or later. Identity, the psychological unity and persistence of one's personality, is a quality that must be acquired in post-adolescence. It is not a matter that gets settled before then, and at thirty years old a person who has not yet established his or her own sense of identity is unlikely ever to do so.

The Bible's oft quoted edict "a time to reap and a time to sow" addresses the same theme, that the seasons of life have their appropriate tasks. Whether we are speaking of biology or psychology, farming, religion, or business, you don't sow in autumn and reap in the spring. In business, research and development must be most intense in the beginning of the life cycle. Fostering market share is, perhaps, the essential task of the growth quarter. It's very costly to increase the market share of a mature product. Cost efficiency is the issue of a mature season in the life of a business.

The four types of business in the famous Boston Consulting Group growth/share matrix of the 1960s and 1970s cor-

2020 VISION

respond to the four life cycle seasons of gestation, growth, maturity, and aging. "Question Marks" were first-season businesses requiring investment for a future payoff, which only some would make. "Stars" were fast growing businesses in the second season. "Cows"—that is, businesses to be milked—were in the third, mature season of the cycle, and "Dogs" were the aging businesses in the fourth season, at the end of their lives. Although the language was rather unkind, it was nevertheless understood that businesses reach the end of useful lives and should be discarded. At the same time, what was never appreciated adequately is that the same thing is true of organizations. Aging organizations are dogs, biting the business hand that feeds them, and should also be discarded. Instead, they hang on, killing the business they are there to serve.

Good housekeeping for young people just out of college is very different from what it will be for them in their suburban homes thirty years later. Similarly, technologists, marketers, manufacturing efficiency specialists, and finance people might be the best rotation of good housekeepers through the life cycle of a business. For a while, in the 1970s, there was even an effort to match personality types of managers to stages in business life cycles.

If you think for a moment about the four seasons, where would you find the venture capitalists? In the first period, of course. Takeover artists? Period four, most likely. Successful entrepreneurs usually play a dominant role in the second season. You can't breed them from the mature end of the life cycle curve. Entrepreneurs must begin their own life cycles to succeed. It hardly seems a coincidence that the entrepreneurial renaissance of the 1970s and 1980s coincided with the second or growth quarter of the current economy. Mature organizations do not, nay, cannot hatch many entrepreneurs.

Young adulthood is the healthiest time to bear offspring—for both people and corporations. The young are resilient and more capable of putting in the hard hours needed for raising the next generation. By the time parents, both human and corporate, are well into middle age, they are more reluctant and much less able to get down in the sandbox and the mud pile with their youngsters.

Executives who accept the mortality of their company are more likely to start bearing and nurturing new companies shortly after their own company has reached adulthood and not wait until it is creaky and paunchy, further into its middle age. Their goal should be that both they and their companies are still healthy and mature when their offspring have themselves arrived at adulthood.

During life's stages of maturity and decline, people occasionally try to change who they are in basic ways; some, for example, start new marriages, new families, new careers. Statistically speaking, however, few of those who do undertake these major transformations attempt them when they are well into their middle or later years. The fortysomething decade is when the "one last chance" feeling occurs. Beyond that, there are few exceptions to the general rule. Companies also attempt a chance at another life, sometimes changing their entire business mix within five or six years. Unlike people, however, companies seem to postpone these attempted transformations until they have lost their vibrancy and are in declining health. Corporate name changes to acronyms never seem to occur during young adulthood, and they suggest that the companies are no longer what they thought they were and that they don't have clarity and commitment about what they will become.

For companies lucky and smart enough to survive through their maturity, old age still comes much sooner than it does for humans. Unlike people, few companies that have been around for twenty years are still thought to be in their growth quarter. More likely, their growth has flattened considerably and they are considered "mature." Very much like people, however, companies seem to want to grow up very quickly and rush through the first half of their life. Then when they finally do reach maturity, they subscribe to the Jack Benny "thirty-nine forever" rule and stretch out the second half as long as possible.

When people do this, we see the self-delusion and smile understandingly, knowing that while the seasons of life may come a little early or a little late, in general they don't vary that much. When companies do this, by contrast, we praise their management. We shouldn't. Executives may be able to say, "Our product line is maturing, and we have to bring out the next generation"; but they seem unable to say, "Our organization is maturing, and we have to phase it out, too, and bring on the next-generation organization to match our new business line." Not many executives are willing to say, "Our organization has lived more than half of its life." One of the best things managers can do for their organization is to let it match their business, and that means with respect to age, too.

A common way for a mature organization to do this is to seed its young businesses with young managers. When Sears started its Discover Card Division, for example, it set up an organization outside of the traditional Sears hierarchy. Most personnel were Sears veterans, but even today the division head is in his thirties, and the average age is less than thirty-five. Less than five years old, Discover Card is the third largest credit card company in the world and the fastest growing division in Sears. AT&T is following the same model.

Aging companies don't go on decade after decade. Either they revitalize their business or they die. But even if they revitalize their business, if they don't also revitalize their organization, they still die. New, second-generation businesses won't run for long with old, first-generation organizations. A corollary is that when change initiatives and revitalization programs focus only on the organization, they are bound to fail. The business has to be revitalized first. Only then should focus shift to organization. Employees in mature companies, who tend to focus more on organization than they should, may kill the business and eventually find themselves unemployed.

■ The Myth of the Immortal Corporation, or How to Manage Your Organization's Life Cycle

Companies don't live as long as people. The average American today has a life expectancy of around seventy-five years, which is about the same probable life span as for the economy itself, but only a very small handful of companies live that long. A major reason is that managers know their businesses have life cycles but deny the equal truth that their organizations also live and die by this same rule. The consequence is that they are able to shed businesses that are at the end of their life cycles and move on to others with a better future, but they cannot do the same thing with their organizations.

People grow up accepting that they will die. Apart from believing in the hereafter, they cope with their own mortality by having children who carry on their lifeline. These same people, however, spend their careers with an opposite assumption about their corporations. While managers accept their own mortality, they wrongheadedly think that they can and should build immortal corporations. They believe in a pervading myth of corporate life: if they all do their jobs right, their company can escape the fate of a life cycle and live on forever. This *myth of the immortal corporation* results in one of our housekeeping ways that gets us into a mess of trouble.

Executives accept the passage from birth to death of civilizations, of types of economies, and of different industries. They accept the beginning and end of individual businesses, and the life cycle of products. Eighty percent of new consumer products, for example, don't survive one year in the marketplace. Why, then, do executives resist the inevitable, absolute mortality of their corporations? It is an unfair, unrealistic, and self-inflicted burden. If they embraced the life cycle process and accepted corporate mortality, they could manage a maturing economy and an older generation of businesses more realistically and prepare better for the next generation. *Companies would live longer and be more successful if the ways they manage and organize were premised on the same life cycles as those of their businesses.*

Does anyone remember Atlas Powder, Bates Manufacturing, and Cuban Atlantic Sugar? They were all part of the first *Fortune* 500 list, in 1955. Less than 35 percent of the original members remain alive today. Forty percent of the 1970 list had vanished by 1985! Some disappeared due to some mortal weakness, others due to mergers and acquisitions between healthy companies for competitive advantage, but that too is a form of corporate death.[3] The New Hampshire state motto, "Live Free or Die," seems an apt expression of the way virtually all managers feel about mergers. Once a company is acquired, like Kaiser by Ford or RCA by GE, it has next to no chance of regaining its original freedom. True, the resources and assets of the original entity exist somewhere, but the entity itself lives only in memories. The high failure rate of LBOs make them less exceptions than exceptions that test the rule. In countries and companies, the loss of freedom ultimately signals the loss of identity.

What, then, can be done to improve the probable life span of corporations? The first thing is to shed the impossible belief and desire for corporate immortality and embrace in its place the reality of the life cycle. Next, explicitly ask and examine how management and organization strategies would differ if we began, instead, with the assumption of absolute corporate mortality. Third, using simple industry data as actuarial tables, assess the infant mortality rates, mid-life coronaries, and probable hardening of the arteries of even well-run corporations in your company's line of work. Ask questions like: "How old is our company? Where do we think that it is in its life cycle? What are we doing to bring forth the next generation of businesses and the next generation of organization?"

People are born with a set of genes that pretty much defines the parameters of their life span. Within this context, their diet, exercise, life-style, and other factors come into play. But the context is given: in Joe's family the men live into their nineties; in Bob's they die in their fifties. Although there is no genetic structure for corporations in a literal sense, it seems reasonable that something analogous does operate, and then it is only within those parameters that a powerful vision, a brilliant strategy, excellent management, and all the other housekeeping factors come into play.

Mortality rates, for example, are far worse for companies than they are for people. Eight out of every ten new companies in the United States fail before age two, whereas seven out of ten children born in the Third World do reach that age. Companies born in the United States have far worse chances of surviving than do babies born in even the most underdeveloped countries. Surely with better housekeeping models we could reduce corporate infant mortality.

Businesses at the beginning of their life cycle tend to be underorganized while those at the mature end of their curve tend to be overorganized. The former almost never use management consultants; the latter use them regularly. Somewhere in the middle of the life cycle curve is a theoretical point where the business and its organization are in proper balance. The organization neither lags nor leads; at that moment, it is in perfect synch. For most, this moment is fleeting. Instead of synchrony between business and organization, the more common state is imbalance.

Are we to believe that finding this equilibrium point and replicating it at all times in the life cycle is the desirable goal? No. The kind of organization appropriate for a start-up is quite different from the one needed for a large, mature company. And a major reason why a mature company is not very good at spawning new businesses is that it often imposes on start-ups the same organizational requirements that it bears. Another reason is the belief that there is a desirable organization profile for each point of development that the business has reached on the life cycle curve. This is like the family member who always tries to make peace but never confronts the source of the conflict.

Companies seldom if ever seem to have their business and organization in balance with each other. Rather than assume perfect match-ups are possible at all points on the life cycle curve, a far more realistic assumption is that perfect match-ups are never possible. One always leads while the other lags, and which one that is shifts somewhere between growth and maturity in but a fleeting moment.

When you ask business people which are the best times,

they always say it is when they are running fast because the business is growing, even while the organization is puffing to keep up. No one says the reverse. So let's posit that this is the healthy state of things, and the reverse is unhealthy. *Businesses should stay just a little bit ahead of their organizations.* This lead-follow relationship should occur throughout the life cycle of the business, but it rarely does. Somewhere in the second half of life, organization seems to catch up with and overtake the business. Bureaucracies grow when an organization's life cycle gets ahead of the life cycle of its business. At their best, organizations should always be lagging no more nor less than a few microseconds behind their businesses.

Greater efficiencies may change the slope of the present curve in the life cycle of the organization, but reorganization, downsizing, consulting reports, and the like won't change the fundamental relationship with the business. Greater effectiveness, by contrast, will only come from determining which new life cycle to pursue. From the corporate point of view, it is time to pursue the next life cycle curve at the first suspicion that the organization tail is wagging the business dog. *Somewhere on the road just past growth and still short of maturity is the best place to start the next generation of both business and organization.*

Managers running older generation businesses should use internal information turbochargers to fight spreading bureaucracy that saps their strength and vitality. Phillips Petroleum, for example, implemented an Executive Information System that enabled the company to reduce its staff to line ratio from 30 percent in 1986 to 13 percent by 1988 and significantly improve its overall performance. At the same time, the job of senior management is to parent new-generation businesses at the front of the next life cycle curve, and to allow those new businesses to create their own forms of organization. In the same mature petroleum industry, ARCO has been leading this move with innovations in its distribution channels, mainly through its highly successful "AM/PM" stores. Because large corporations generally have a very poor record of creating new businesses with their own organizations, however, something fundamentally different must be done with their models.

■ Match the Life Cycle of an Organization to the Life Cycle of Its Business

Why do executives accept life cycle realities in their business, but reject a parallel reality in their organization? An organization will never be more sprightly than the business it serves. A prerequisite for mature companies wanting to redesign and recreate their organizations, therefore, is for them to start on successful new business life cycles. A business and its organization are a couple, and when one is much younger than the other, as with people, May-December marriages can be far from ideal for obvious reasons. No one knows what wine to order with the peanut butter.

There is something sad and misplaced about large, very mature corporations dreaming of creating organizations that will always be young and vibrant. You can't have young and vibrant organizations without young and vibrant businesses to run, and you rarely find old and sagging businesses run by young and vibrant organizations. *If the management can't invigorate the business, it shouldn't waste its time attempting to invigorate its organization.* This view is heretical and offensive only for those who operate within an immortality framework.

The best match-ups between a business and an organization are when the life cycles of the two are as closely parallel as a company can get them to be. Young entrepreneurs often grow exciting and chaotic organizations, and the two seem to share the exhilaration, awkwardness, and pain of adolescent marriage. The faster a business moves from conception through growth, the more difficult it is to have the organization keep pace. The last thing a young business needs is an overly developed organization ahead of its time, and it is equally bad for the organization not to keep pace with rapid business growth.

Sun Microsystems is a typical example of the problems

that can occur when a company's organization does not keep up with its business growth. Sun was responsible for some fundamental changes in the computer industry while, at the same time, it grew from $0 to $2 billion and from four people to ten thousand in seven years. "Things in Sun over the last seven years always seemed, if not out of control, at least right on the edge," says Crawford Beveridge, vice president for corporate resources. "New people often found a lack of rules and structure that they would have expected in a company of the size we were becoming. Typically, there was some overlap and some underlap. Our conclusion, even if we were always behind in the hiring curve, was to hire people who deal easily with first principles, a few rules, and a lot of ambiguity."

Like a marriage, a company will succeed best when its two partners, business and organization, pass through the same seasons of their lives more together than apart. There is a fit and a logic to closely matched pairs. Although it is difficult to accomplish, *the most effective organization is one that is matched to the same point in its life cycle as the business it serves.*

It is not easy, once an organization infrastructure has been fixed, to shed it completely for another one. Crustaceans grow exoskeletons and shed their shells in order to grow. Corporations can't do this. Instead, their organizations grow like endoskeletons and suffer all the pains of aging bodies that cannot be shed even if they no longer do what their management wants them to do. Companies are limited to only semi-satisfying reconstructive surgery, called "reorganization," and to liposuction, called "downsizing," where they take out extra layers of management around the middle but leave the basic form the same. Companies that need tummy tucks are not in prime condition for raising offspring.

A more effective approach may not involve losing extra weight so much as transforming unhealthy fat into healthy muscle and other tissue. A first step in this direction, in corporate housekeeping terms, is repositioning people into more productive jobs, wherever possible, rather than laying them off. A popular and successful method for doing this in mature companies is to move staff people into sales jobs. IBM and AT&T are two of the companies that have done this in recent years.

IBM had always prided itself on meeting its customers' needs, but when its near monopoly eroded and its growth consistently slipped, in the late 1980s, it finally underwent a massive reorganization. Commenting on what went wrong, CEO John Akers said, "We were trying to solve some problems that were more IBM's than the customer's." Because of its no-layoff tradition, downsizing through early retirement only eliminated 6,500 people from the payroll. More important, Akers moved 20,000 people from staff and labs to sales, increasing both revenues and customer contact.

AT&T's $14 billion corporate long-distance business transferred 5,500 staffers into sales jobs in 1989. According to the sales-oriented head of the operation, Joseph Nacchio, the move recaptured several hundred million dollars in revenues. Paine Webber, as an example, asked MCI, US Sprint, and AT&T for proposals for cheaper and faster ways to link their stockbrokers with information about their customer accounts. With over a dozen salespeople and pricing analysts working on the project within twenty-four hours, and a plan in forty-four days to save the client $1 million a month, AT&T won the account before the others had even responded.

Nobody has zero body fat, although the most top-notch conditioning does get some athletes down to 2 or 3 percent. Most men, by contrast, carry around 15–18 percent body fat, and women lug around 25–28 percent. In the corporate world, mature companies, like mature people, tend to put on weight. People diet and exercise to stay healthy, which suggests that corporations might take a similar approach toward conditioning their organizations. Staff is like fat, a little is necessary and healthy, a lot is the opposite. Most bodies, both corporate and individual, however, have much more than they need. While virtually no company will ever get to zero staff, that isn't a bad focus to take. Conditioning may help them lead longer and more productive lives; still, the fact remains they cannot live forever.

Aging ball players don't get younger; they become

coaches, managers, sportscasters, and advertising personalities. The professional life span of most athletes is well under two decades, except in the rarest of cases. Those who continue successful careers beyond that are able to do so because they switched their business mix so thoroughly. Arnold Palmer stayed in business because he changed the business he was in. But many others merely try to extend their sports life cycle, rather than create another one of comparable worth.

When thoroughbreds can no longer race, they are still valuable as studs. Why do we resist the aging process in corporations? Why do we try to keep decrepit ones racing? Denial of death can kill you.

▪ Grow and Reproduce, or Die

Economies of scale help big mature corporations to survive competition, but at the far end of this scale they experience diseconomies of size. Here they grow to the point where they are unmanageable. The housekeeping rules break down. They stop growing, and any living thing that stops growing begins dying. So large companies either die, which may take decades, or they evolve a new form, a new logic capable of organizing and administering growth cycles at a higher level of complexity.

There are only two ways to keep companies from dying: through growth and reproduction, both extensions through time and space. While growth is the key to life within a single life cycle, reproduction is the key to life across a succession of life cycles. Living things can grow only if they continue to differentiate themselves internally, but that too has limitations. There are limits to the logic of any design. Growth ends when you reach those limits; maturity begins and eventually there is decline. To be able to continue to grow, the entity has to figure out a new logic, a new pattern or design. *Once you've reached a design limit, to continue growing you have to redefine the very entity itself.*

The evolution of species, the creation of nation states from city states, and all manner of individual accomplishments speak to such redefinitions. The technological shift from analog to digital and the transformation from agrarian to industrial economies are additional examples. As information-age businesses mature, it is increasingly apparent that industrial-age housekeeping models have reached their design limits. We have to redesign the organization.

There have been many organizational conversions to support new levels of business growth beyond the limits of an earlier design. The product division structure, developed by General Motors in the 1920s, enabled corporations to grow larger by a putting-together, by figuring out how to multiply the functional structure severalfold. The strategic business unit concept, pioneered by General Electric thirty years later, enhanced growth by moving in the opposite direction, a taking-apart, by searching for the smallest complete business unit in an ever smaller whole.

Another thirty years later, led by companies like McDonald's, the explosive growth of franchising offered another major organizational innovation. The current slowing of the rate of growth of franchising is probably one reflection of the economy's shift into its mature third quarter. Franchising earned a very mixed reputation during this boom period, when many people with only the most half-baked business ideas used it as a flimflam to bilk people into making poor investments. But as an organizing principle it has certainly bested any other approach in beating business infant mortality statistics. Although not applicable to all businesses, franchising clearly must be added to the list of good housekeeping ways in the information age.

One might also redesign the organization by thinking of companies growing and reproducing like plants that send out runners. Runners start little plants, growing their own leaves and roots, but they are still attached to the parent plant. In the beginning, the umbilical cords that connect them are more prominent than the little offshoots at the ends. The new little start-ups are complete plants, yet initially they depend upon the parent plant for source and resourcing. As the new plants put out roots, searching for soil to anchor in, there is a clear intention to establish their own viability and independence. They have moved from undeveloped beginnings through growth to maturity. When a runner is cut, for whatever reason, an established newer plant is clearly its own whole, and depending on when the separation takes place, it may or may not be viable as an independent entity.

This is the logic that is used in spin-off businesses, such as the new generation of information service businesses. They start as protected newborns, supplied by the parent. Once they are viable, they generate their own resources. They may be smaller, equal, or larger than the parent. They may stay attached to the parent or be sold off. When the core business is not doing well, the runner-businesses will send food to the parent, and the whole larger ecosystem stays in place.

If the runner plant remains attached to the parent plant, is it another plant or isn't it? It is both, depending on how it is perceived. Similarly, divisions and strategic business units in a diversified corporation are both wholes and parts of larger wholes. If you leave a viable business inside the company, it is both a whole and a part simultaneously. The more apart it is, the less it is a part. But as a separate whole, it is less than when it is simultaneously whole and part. The information-based businesses we have been discussing, particularly in their early stages, are just such cases. Sabre, for example, may have an extremely high breakaway value for Wall Street analysts, but it is worth more to its parent by remaining attached as both whole and part.

The whole-part connection extends an entity's life in both time and space. Green plants and businesses that operate this way get both bigger and smaller simultaneously, and consequently they live longer in the bargain. They get smaller because they are constantly starting new entities and larger because they stay connected to each other. They are operating on several life cycle curves at once. Successfully managing growth and greater complexity this way means connecting to a living network, being both whole and part simultaneously. What makes the network a form of organization that can sustain greater size and complexity is that it is premised on the whole-part simultaneity.

The models that will emerge for the housekeeping of information-age organizations are the ones that have what scientists now refer to as the whole-part quality of *self-similarity*. That is, *any part is like the whole, and vice versa*. Go up to a higher level of organization, and the earlier whole now looks like the same part repeated over and over. Go down to a lower level of organization, and parts behave similarly to the whole. This model of organization utilizes a self-replicating pattern, up and down the scale.

Scientists are able to demonstrate this self-similarity mathematically, as in the fractal geometry of snowflakes, coastlines, anatomy, and all structures in nature. Science is already finding practical application, as in the reduction of heart attacks through drugs that treat arrhythmia, and is seeking application to economic phenomena, such as determining patterns in seemingly erratic price swings in the stock market. Those who would apply it to organization design, however, must still use it in a simpler form, as image rather than equation. Here are two applications, one up and one down the scale of business organization.

■ Build Your *Inter*Organization

First, up the scale. We are moving into an organizational world that is increasingly *inter*organizational rather than *intra*organizational. Because of information technology, the organization is becoming electronically linked, upstream to its suppliers, downstream through distributors to customers, and laterally in global and strategic alliances. Despite the emerging electronic technology, companies have not yet developed models to manage the interorganizational linkages. Instead, most take the organization as the universe. All considerations and efforts to manage and change it are internal, focused on what goes on within the boundaries of the company. We are particularly uncomfortable with the notion of *housekeeping*—keeping more than one house—a term that would describe an *inter*organization model.

We've heard the term *inter*organization for a decade, and while we see the phenomenon increasing, no one has gotten very excited about it. Whether intra-O or inter-O, each term is still a mouthful and neither is particularly sonorous or glamorous. If only we had a more catchy expression for interorganization, we might be able to implement the reality sooner. Instead, we spend incredible amounts of money, energy, and time trying to pull off all sorts of organizational change, and with very poor results. Why? Because we are encumbered by very mature, highly articulated *intra*organizational models. And like the mature businesses and industries they were built around, they resist change or concentrate their efforts on refining, rather than redefining, their function.

The *inter*organizational world, by contrast, is absolutely virgin territory. There is little understanding of the fact that the return on interorganization investment is much greater than on that for changes in intraorganization. Try this: Out of every dollar spent on organization changes, apply twenty cents to develop interorganizational linkages. You'll get a much better return on your investment, as well as on the psychological and conceptual energies involved. These linkages don't have to be inventive, creative, or cutting edge. Just take a lot of the activities that already exist within your organization and start to apply them to the linkages between your company and others. Here are examples from three functions: R&D, Distribution, and Human Resources.

Current organization models have always emphasized the importance and difficulties of coordinating R&D efforts with other functional departments inside the company, an intraorganizational concern. Now, managers know that they have to coordinate R&D directly with the customer, an interorganizational concern. "Your competition will be tailoring products even before they finish inventing them," say Ira Magaziner and Mark Patinkin. "It's becoming a common strategy to work with customers while you're still in the

R&D lab. . . . The only way to beat [the competition] will be to get customers advising you in the lab while you're still experimenting."[4]

As businesses link up- and downstream, the need for interorganization management also increases. Every one connected becomes more of a distribution business, linking players in a value chain. Over the next decade, therefore, we must look for opportunities to develop the distribution and delivery aspects of our *housekeeping*.

Within the Human Resources function, there are many activities that can be linked interorganizationally: reporting relationships, compensation systems, controls, and training programs, for example. Reserve twenty percent of the seats in every in-house training program for suppliers, distributors, and customers. Beyond the endless debate about monies kept by the divisions versus those tithed to the center, create interorganizational models that also include suppliers, distributors, and customers in sharing the pot.

▪ A New Design Limit: Each Employee Equals a Business

Interorganization models are typically applied up the scale to the company as a whole, in all its size and complexity. They can also be applied down the scale, within the smallest possible unit, even to single individuals in the company, making them into true entrepreneurs.

When business units get too big they became unwieldly. Successful companies find ways to break them up before diseconomies of scale set in. Strategic business units (SBUs) have become a way to organize around the smallest possible complete business. Companies that are lauded for this innovative behavior, such as Johnson & Johnson and 3M, might have business units as large as four thousand employees, but also as small as fifteen. If fifteen is viable, why not five, or even one? The ultimate logic is that each employee is potentially a business.

Remember that the basic idea is to shift the focus from organization to business. Some companies have done that by moving staff personnel into sales positions to regain their business focus. Here, we are pushing the notion even further by transferring all staff into a line activity, each operating with a profit and loss statement as a complete business. In this system, all employees must earn their own way. If their services are wanted, they will be paid for. No activity is chalked up to overhead, and nothing is provided for free. If you want mail delivered, you pay for using the mailroom; if you want your bathrooms cleaned, you pay for that.

Clerical, maintenance, and support work of this nature is generally lumped together under an accounting category called General Administration, with a percentage of budget assessed to cover the costs. This may be rational, but it is also self-defeating. Initially, it simplifies things greatly. Stationery, cafeterias, security, and a hundred and one other necessities are grouped together for both accounting and management ease. Historically, the chores were taken care of rather painlessly for only a nominal fee of about 10 to 15 percent of budget. As long as these costs were nominal, they didn't require much attention. Today, they are double or triple that in most businesses. They should be "deregulated" from their internal imprisonment. That is, they should be made into businesses. *The conversion of organization into business always strengthens corporate performance.*

This is already being done today, in a variant on the make-versus-buy decision. When companies decide that it is cheaper to buy something than to make it, they contract an outside supplier. In this manner, Marriott Foods might be called on to run the cafeteria, Pitney-Bowes to operate the mailroom, Brinks to provide security, Bankers Trust to collect receivables, and so on.

Why not contract these activities to the very people who run them now? Make employees into entrepreneurs who have legal and economic ownership of the business for which they are responsible. When the focus of a corporation is on internal organization, the only way to gain importance is to build your staff and budget, and since internal administrations run as monopolies, that isn't hard to do. When the model focuses on the businesses, that is, the customer in the marketplace, the way to gain importance is through profitable customer service. *When the focus shifts from organization to business, internal "customers" become real customers, and the level of service improves.*

This approach will increase slowly over the next decade. Today, only the outline of the concept is visible. But like archaeologists examining tomorrow instead of yesterday, we can piece together the "shards" of future organizations. Let's imagine that your company is setting up this new housekeeping rule of the game. You will only hire people who are willing to set themselves up in business. Here's the deal. They can open up businesses with themselves as the only employee to provide your company with a specific service. The business is jointly owned by them and the parent company, which initially is their financial backer and sole customer. If they are successful, there is a phased buy-out plan so that eventually they become the dominant owner. Each year they are allowed to sell an agreed percent of their services on the open market. To get started, however, they have a guaranteed market.

Many people in large companies would rather be employees than entrepreneurs. The idea is to structure a model that allows them to be either. Take secretaries, for example. Not all of them will like or understand this arrangement. But the plan will attract those who do, and every twentieth or hundredth secretary may start another Kelly Girls. Can't you imagine one of them grasping the idea and then franchising the other secretarial slots within the company? Two or three might consolidate the market by buying up the others. Specializations might develop. One might focus on desktop publishing, another on travel bookings, and a third on the meetings and seminars business. The effect would be revolutionary.

The social consequences of such an economic organization would be democratizing. Traditionally, the people who perform service jobs have always been given lower status. Staff is to corporations what domestics are to a wealthy family. The place may not run without them, but they are not the ones the place runs for. Nor are low-status roles always limited to peripheral activities. All businesses have their back and front lines. The frontline jobs are generally the glory and gravy. The ones in back are generally the grind and grit. If a brokerage house or investment banking firm sold its back office to the partner who ran it, that person might become as rich and respected as the more visible traders and dealmakers out front.

Clearly, such a step would unleash a great deal of energy. There are great risks, and management would unleash a tiger that it would then have to ride. The ultimate outcome would not be clear. Premature reaction to the turbulence might squash the whole idea. A disorderly experiment with modernizing organization might result in an even more conservative regime than before the exploration for new ways began. In this century, it has happened many times to many nations—and to many companies. A few succeeded, many failed.

According to one comedian, the members of Congress have been unable to balance the budget and show a profit for two hundred years, so his solution is to put them on commission. California, Florida, Pennsylvania, and Tennessee have privatized some of their prisons, and such experiments might measure success by decreasing costs and lowering recidivism. The town of Chelsea, Massachusetts, handed its school system over to Boston University. These are experiments that go to the core of organization structure and design. They question the most fundamental assumptions and deal with the underlying social philosophy. They are moved to do so only because the changed economic realities make the existing models impossible.

The Swedish tax system has provided just such an incentive, creating organization structures that lead to both more effective business performance and increased personal income. Personal income taxes in Sweden go to as high as 75 or 80 percent, making it very difficult for companies to motivate employees to work harder or longer. When virtually all additional earnings go to taxes, people opt for leisure rather than more work. Corporate tax laws, however, are very good in Sweden, and very few companies pay more than 30 percent in taxes. There are also a lot of possibilities to set profits aside in reserved "funds." When you sell a company, taxes are due on only 40 percent of the capital gain after two years, which is much better than paying a personal income tax of 75 percent.

The inadvertent effect has been to flatten the organization pyramid and to increase entrepreneurship and customer service in most companies. Antonson-Security, in Stockholm, manufactures and sells electronic anti-shoplifting systems, mainly to department and hardware stores and supermarkets. There were some twelve people in the sales organization, all working on a fixed salary plus a 15 to 20 percent bonus. "They were an expensive fixed cost, and not motivated enough," says Anders Ilstam, then chairman. "They made too few calls, stayed in too-expensive hotels, and so on. The sales cost for the company was 18 percent. We then formed a company where the twelve salesmen owned 60 percent of the shares and the company owned 40 percent. An agreement regulated sales volumes and a normal agency agreement was made. They got a 15 percent commission on the sales, so the company was already 3 percent better off. The guys suddenly turned around and sold like never before, made a lot of money for themselves as well as for the company, used their own company to assume a lot of their private costs, and the expense accounts dropped. They took out a much lower salary but started to build up an equity in the company in the form of leasing contracts, etc. Later, we found that it would have been better to form two companies with six salesmen each. Too big a group could create problems."

Trygg Hansa, a large Swedish insurance company, extended this logic further some years ago. They put all their salesmen, over a hundred, in one-person companies. These sales-entrepreneurs leased office, administration, and bookkeeping from the parent and lived on commission only. They got results similar to the security company's—fixed costs transferred to variable, and higher output—and everybody was happy.

If an accounting department costs the company 3 percent of sales to run, sell it to the accountants for that same amount. Chances are, they will find ways to offer the same quality of accounting for 2 percent, giving the accountant-entrepreneurs the freedom to invest the 1 percent difference in product development, office furnishings, equity, or whatever, and at a much better tax advantage.

Mr. Ilstam, now the chief executive of SKF Tools, says, "I cannot see any reason why a company could not consist of any number of privately owned companies servicing the main organization." He also thinks about driving this concept both up and out of the company, as well as down the hierarchy. In a letter, he writes:

> Maybe two or three presidents or CEOs could form a company and sell their services to their corporations. Let me play with the thought! The CEO makes $200,000 US plus car, etc., plus 56 percent benefits to be paid by the company; in total, some $350,000 USD. The company will now pay the same amount to the CEO's "consulting" company, from which he will draw only a moderate salary of $50,000 USD. This will cost his company only $80–90,000 USD, with [perks and] benefits, and he will end up having more than $200,000 USD in the company to invest, build equity, and maybe give his wife a salary. This is not bad! Soon, we will probably find a lot more flexible organization patterns that could suit everybody.

American managers should learn from these examples, without having to experience the incentives of a 75 percent personal income tax.

■ How It's Going to Happen

Agriculture is the oldest and most capital-intensive sector of the economy today. The industrial sector is second. Services are the least capital-intensive. Similarly, within companies, the factory is more so than the office, but the office will become more capital-intensive as this economy matures and will catch up with factories in the second half of this economy. Moreover, for every dollar spent in that now technologically expensive office, several additional dollars will be spent on intangible human and administrative costs. When the General Administration category of a company budget starts pushing the 40 and 50 percent marks, managers will begin to tinker with the underlying philosophy of organization.

Deregulation, privatization, employee stock ownership plans, unbundling, and decapitalization are such examples, and they all have a common thread in organizational direction: they *focus on the underlying business philosophy and eliminate organization features and procedures that get between the individual and the business.* As we restructure the entire economy and various industries within it, we will, inescapably, also come to restructure the organizations of which they are composed. As with governments, companies will slowly try new ways, and a few ideas will succeed, creating new housekeeping models for a by then mature economy.

The most important housekeeping models in any economy tend to come from the most important economic sector and from its core product. In each economy, the core business influences the way all businesses are conducted, and the way all organizations are managed. Railroads were at the core of the early industrial economy, for example, and it is the railroad companies that first made the distinction between functional activities and managerial ones. Later, automobiles proved to be the core industry in the industrial economy, and the major forms of management and organization evolved in the automobile industry: Ford's assembly line and Sloan's G.M. structure of centralized planning and control and decentralized operations within divisions.

The organization models we have today were developed in, by, and for industrial corporations. Industrial manufacture, however, represents less than a quarter of our total economy. So the models, even if updated, pertain to an earlier economy. We are using factory-based models to run organizations in an office-based economy. That makes as little sense as using farm models to run a factory economy. Inappropriate management and organization will shorten the life of any company. Our companies would live longer today if our housekeeping methods were more closely modeled on the businesses they are being asked to run.

Information, the key driver of this economy, will increasingly influence the way we manage, organize, and source the future models for good housekeeping. It is already clear that information is having an enormous impact on the way all business is conducted. Over the next few decades it will become clear that information technology and the information sector of business will also have an impact on the housekeeping of these businesses, that is, on their management and organization. For the past decade their impact has been felt as metaphor; during the coming decade the linkage between information and organization will become more literal.

Networks are a case in point. The sequence in which they will evolve is from technological networks, to business networks, to organization networks. We already speak easily about the old and new organization models as the *shift from hierarchies to networks*, as if networked organizations were currently a real possibility rather than a mere image. Until the technological networks are in place, however, networked businesses are still expectations more than realities. And both the technological and business models precede the organizational ones. Networked organizations, as actualities rather than possibilities, therefore, must wait their turn. We are all anxious for their day to come, and when it does it will launch organizations onto a new life cycle. Then, at least for a time, our housekeeping ways will suit our house. Until then there will be a mismatch and a lag, companies with information-age businesses run with industrial-age methods, a mismatch that shortens companies' lives.

Another major issue in information technology, besides networks, is expressed by the currency of words like "seamless" and "transparent." They address the importance of getting incompatible computer systems to hook up with one another, to connect. "Connectivity" is a byword of the 1990s. All the black boxes have to connect with each other into networks, and local area networks (LANs) have to connect with wide area networks (WANs). The connections cannot be cumbersome patch jobs. They have to be smooth, invisible, effortless, continuous. In the old lingo, the telephone company might have "patched" you into the line, but in the new economy you must no longer see even the seams on the patch.

In the early decades of the automobile, users had to be fairly knowledgeable about the mechanics of the thing. You had to know how to crank the motor to start it and how to fix and tinker with it to keep it going. Only a few decades later, most people no longer wanted to know how it worked, nor did they know how to fix it; they only wanted to drive it. Computers are at the same crossover point today. People don't want to know how they work; they would much rather be able to use them without having to know. What is true for automobiles and computers probably will also be true for organizations.

Organizations need to become seamless and transparent. Just as computer firms are stepping up efforts to make their machines easier to use, management must also step up its efforts to make organizations easier to use. The reason organizations get so much remedial attention is that they are not easy to use. Like early cars and computers, they are cumbersome, and most people only care how they work, if they have to, in order to fix them. And for good reasons, they would much rather use them than understand them. *Like computers, successful organizations must learn to be easy to use, friendly, seamless, and transparent.*

Communicating with a computer is still not easy for the majority of people. If computers are supposed to make life easier, why are most of them so hard to use? Only when they become easy and fun will they fulfill the promise of the computer visionaries who use phrases like "wings for the mind." Until then, they weigh you down. Organizations that fit the needs and take advantage of the potentials of this economy will have to make the same shift and become easier to use. Like yesterdays' computers, today's organizations are still weights, not wings. Tomorrow's organizations will have to be lifters.

Aware of these limitations, and perceiving the directions in which we are headed, we have adjusted our models and now stress the need for our organizations to become *"flat," "flexible," and built around "teams."* But this is about as far as we have gotten with a new reality, and while such moves are in the right direction, they are merely adjustments to the old model, rather than fundamental rethinking based on the differences between the industrial and information economies.

We face an organization conundrum. The old models don't work, and the new ones have yet to evolve. What do we do in the meanwhile? The straightforward answer is, focus far more on your business than on your organization. As old businesses give way to new ones in the inevitable cycle of destruction and creation, so too will their organizations. Don't prop them up. Let them go gently into the dark night of organizational mortality.

CHAPTER 5

You Can't Ride on Tracks
You Haven't Laid Down

*Toto, I have a feeling we're not in Kansas
anymore.*

Dorothy, in The Wizard of Oz

Woody Allen once asked Arnold Schwarzenegger how long it would take him to build a body like Arnold's. "About two generations," was the reply. It also takes about that long to lay the infrastructure, the bones and muscles, of a powerful economy. New economies don't just happen. They are built by visionaries.

The Sagres Institute was established in 1419 to promote Portuguese leadership in shipbuilding, navigation, mapping, and other seafaring sciences. Located at the southern tip of the Iberian Peninsula in the town of Sagres, this state-sponsored center built the technological foundation for an economy based on global marine commerce. Its technicians designed galleons and navigation systems that created an empire spanning oceans and centuries.

Portugal initiated the era of global marine commerce, but that economy did not reach its full potential in Iberia. The ultimate models and institutions were British. Just as the mercantile economy originated in Portugal and peaked in Britain, in turn, the industrial economy that began in England peaked in the United States.

The information economy originated in the United States, but will it reach its highest point there? Will the ultimate models and institutions be American? Many Americans believe that the United States has locked in a dominant position in the core information technologies and industries of today's economy. They are in for a rude shock.

In the second half of this economy, international competitiveness will be built on computers and telecommunications. American leadership in these sectors is by no means secure. Nations both large and small are developing technologies, promoting industries, and building infrastructures to drive superior economic performance. An intense international rivalry is taking shape, and the stakes are nothing less than global economic, military, and political leadership.

No nation can sustain a superior military profile without a superior economy. That is a central issue in the Gorbachev era in the Soviet Union and a growing issue in the United States. The challenge for both the United States and the Soviet Union is quite clear. Future economic and military leadership, social welfare, and general progress hinge on national performance in the information technologies. *Sustained dominance of core information technologies and industries is the critical platform for future world leadership.*

The United States has competed with specialized rivals in the past decades on two fronts: on the military front with the U.S.S.R. and on the economic front with Japan. While the United States fought on both fronts, each of its rivals focused on only one. The Soviet Union concentrated its resources and energies on the military arena and neglected industrial pursuits. Restricted by treaty from rebuilding its military, Japan focused its resources and energies on economic objectives. Our rivalry with the Soviets is now all but over. Without an economic base, the Soviet military position could not be sustained. But the United States is still struggling with its economic adversary. Over the next decade it will more likely be economic competition than military rivalry that determines world leadership. Commercial technologies will be the focus of this competition.

Even before the extraordinary changes began in the U.S.S.R. and Eastern Europe, Japanese commentators understood the power of technology in the realignment of world leadership:

> The forces changing the world today are basically technological, not military or political. Military rivalries are essentially obsolete. The tumultuous military confrontations between the U.S. and the U.S.S.R. have no essential meaning as far as the logic of history is concerned. Military and political forces can be reduced fundamentally to economic forces, and economics are based on technology. The world moves in whatever direction is dictated by technology, and the power of technology to change the world will become

increasingly strong in the future. The world's geopolitical axes will converge more and more at the location where the new technology reigns. That center of convergence is, of course, Japan.[1]

We do not agree that military power is irrelevant, even though the industrial basis for it can become obsolete. Human history suggests that military rivalries won't disappear. The technology of warfare just evolves. Economic and political power can be had in the future only if leadership is maintained in those technologies and industries that are crucial to *both* fronts. In the near term, however, the United States can afford to shift resources from the arms race to the economic race. In fact, if it does not redirect its resources toward commercial competition in core information technologies and industries, it will lose both races.

By the end of this decade, it should be clear who will control the sources of economic and military leadership for the next three or four decades. Microelectronics, computers, and telecommunications are areas where Americans have set the pace, but the prospects for continued American leadership in these technologies and industries are uncertain. Meanwhile, Europe and Japan are investing massive resources to prepare themselves for the second half of this economy.

■ Japan As Information Samurai

A book entitled *Building a New Japan* appeared in the early 1970s.[2] It described a vision of Japan as an information archipelago bound together by sophisticated networks of computer and communications technologies. Similar books have appeared in other nations, but this one is unusual because it was written by Prime Minister Kakuei Tanaka of Japan, a very powerful and pragmatic politician. His book is not considered a work of futuristic fiction, but a widely accepted vision of the nation's destiny. The information economy and society described in his book is actively being developed as a matter of public policy. Japan's leaders aim to do nothing less than rebuild the entire economy on a new infrastructure of information technologies, an effort that is taking visible shape in dozens of communities around the archipelago today. A host of historic infrastructure projects are being implemented in Japan.

On a verdant plain near the ancient Japanese capital city of Kyoto, for example, a new city is taking shape. It will be a city of the twenty-first century, a showcase for the new Japan. Over $20 billion will be planted there to grow a center for science and technology development. Kansai Science City, as it is called, will become home to thousands of researchers and scientists engaged in building the technology base for Japan's postindustrial economy. The first of many Kansai research facilities opened in 1988. Called the Advanced Telecommunications Research Center, it is engaged in advanced computer and communications research. The quiet work of the men and women in this new city may have a great deal of impact on the shape of the next century.

Kansai Science City is but one among dozens of new initiatives currently under way in Japan. In its *Vision for the 1980's*, the Ministry of International Trade and Industry (MITI) proposed a massive national program to deploy advanced information technologies and services in a number of "informationalized cities." Nineteen cities have since been selected as "Technopolis" sites. In each location, advanced computer and communications infrastructures are being installed to stimulate the growth of new information-based businesses and to transform the existing economy and society.

MITI is not alone as a champion of the information infrastructure. The Ministry of Posts and Telecommunications announced its Teletopia Program in 1985, and more than seventy communities have since been approved as sites under this program. The Teletopia Program encompasses a wide range of projects categorized as Telecommunications Plazas, Parks, Teleports, and Teletopia Regions.

The Suwa model community project is a typical Teletopia Region. The Suwa system includes three cities, two towns, and a village connected by an optic fiber network.

The network provides a computer LAN, cable TV, automatic meter reading, farming support services, voter registration, and many other services to the region. The first Telecom Park is the forementioned Advanced Telecommunications Research facility in Kansai Science City. This single facility, which will house a dozen or more research organizations, entails an investment of approximately $750 million.

Another Teletopia project that resides within a larger initiative is the Osaka Teleport, which includes a 3,000-kilometer optic fiber ring that provides the Osaka region with high-speed information connections. This Teleport, completed at a cost of about $300 million in 1989, provides critical support to the larger Osaka Technoport project. The Technoport calls for investment of $16 billion in new facilities to house informationalized industries, including value-added networks and data base, software, telemarketing, and information services. A similar project now under way, the Tokyo Teleport, carries an even larger price tag. Vast resources are being committed to build the infrastructure for Japan's information economy.

The Ministry of Posts and Telecommunications 1989 report stated, "From now until the 21st century, the info-communications foundation must be rapidly reconstructed and spread throughout the nation. Japan needs to become a core country for multi-use info-communication networks." Japan's economic and social agenda rests squarely on this new infrastructure, and it is committing massive resources in laying tracks to the future. These infrastructure investments will support the development of informationalized businesses and communities. Just as smart companies will displace their traditional competitors in the information economy, smart communities and nations will leave their less progressive peers behind. We may end up eating Japan's dust.

Japan is also aggressively promoting the growth of critical information industries. It intends to be the principal source of the feeder technologies and services that will drive the new economy. The formidable machinery of national industrial policy is focusing on this target. Between 1945 and 1970, industrial policy centered on heavy manufacturing industries. Success in three industries—steel, shipbuilding, and automobiles—captured over 40 percent of all capital investment during this period and fed other industrial pursuits. In the 1970s, as the emphasis shifted from survival to leadership, Japan began to target the extended information technology sector.

Public support for the information sector takes many forms in Japan. A principal source of financial support is the Japan Development Bank. The JDB, standing in the inner sanctum of the Japanese economic system, offers preferential loans to strategic development projects. In the mid-1970s, the JDB provided over $400 million in "loans" to the VLSI Project, a consortium of six well-known electronics companies, MITI, and Nippon Telegraph and Telephone (NTT).

The VLSI Project was dedicated to creating state-of-the-art semiconductor memory chip technology in Japan. It was a spectacular success. Japanese firms were the first to introduce commercially the 16K Random Access Memory (RAM) chip, and today they control over 80 percent of the world "merchant" market for semiconductor memory chips. In just ten years, Japanese firms achieved a level of dominance in this critical technology that far surpasses their success in steel, ships, or cars. In the decade of the 1980s, memory chips moved from a capacity of 16,000 bits to 16,000,000 bits, as Japanese firms forced the pace of innovation and obsolescence.

The VLSI Project has become a model for organizing development efforts in other information technologies. Consortiums composed of key companies and public agencies jointly develop key technologies with the assistance of public funding. Some of these projects, like the VLSI effort, receive preferential support in the form of *hojokin* loans from the JDB. Hojokin loans are interest-free, and the principal is forgiven if the project fails. Other projects are funded directly through the federal budget under accounts such as the

Special Account for Industrial Investment. Among the many information technology projects under way in Japan, several deserve special mention.

The TRON project is aimed at the microprocessor segment. Microprocessors, the brains for electronic devices and systems, control everything from smart appliances to the most advanced computers or military systems. This segment has been a virtual American monopoly since the first microprocessor was created by Intel in the early 1970s. TRON aims to establish a Japanese microprocessor technology at the leading edge of the industry.

The Optoelectronics Project also targets critical new technologies. The entire electronics industry uses the electron as the medium for information processing. Optoelectronic devices use photons instead of electrons. Photons could become the core element in the information economy, and Japanese researchers, aggressively exploring this promising new field, have already produced a one-kilobit photonic memory chip. Japan also holds a very strong position in the fiber-optic cable industry. By the time the information economy has matured, its nervous system will be formed by fiber optic cables that use photons to carry and process information at the speed of light.

Another of the foundations of the current electronics industry is silicon. Virtually all semiconductor devices have been built in silicon, and electronic functions today are driven by electrons flowing through silicon. Japan is actively exploring alternative materials. In particular, gallium arsenide (GaAs) is now being widely used in Japan. GaAs devices generate less heat and permit electron emitters and receivers to be located much closer together. Greater proximity means faster processing speed—as much as four or five times faster—and that translates into much greater performance. In certain applications, that speed difference is crucial. In military applications, the speed advantage means the difference between winning and losing in every electronic contest.

Shintaro Ishihara, one of the candidates for the post of Japan's prime minister in 1989, made the often-quoted statement that "If Japan told Washington it would no longer sell computer chips to the United States, the Pentagon would be totally helpless. Furthermore, the global military balance could be completely upset if Japan decided to sell its computer chips to the Soviet Union instead of the United States."[3] The U.S. military dependence is actually very limited, however, and of less concern than growing commercial dependence. But one point is clear. Japan's rising microelectronics prowess addresses a key piece of the platform needed to build an information economy. It is aggressively developing other key elements as well, and its greatest strength may lie in the personal electronics arena.

Japanese firms dominate the consumer audio and video electronics markets. They are strong contenders in the mass markets for printers, disc drives, optical scanners, mobile phones, and copiers. Their niche positions begin to add up to a critical mass, especially when these diverse activities can be integrated into a single package. Already, executives in Japan are offered a smart briefcase that includes a copier, fax, mobile phone, scanner, video link, and a personal computer with printer. Such offerings can only become more integrated, inexpensive, and effective.

We can expect a flood of sophisticated personal electronic devices from Japan in the decades to come, many employing significant new technologies. Japan's most significant opportunity may exist in the audio arena, because of a major disadvantage inherent in Japanese society: its language. The typical text for Japanese is a blend of Kanji, Hiragana, and two other unique alphabets, Katakana and Romanji. Japanese firms are meticulous in documenting meetings and minutiae, most of it stored in warehouses full of paper files. Considering the cost of space in Japan, and the availability of advanced data storage devices, this is a primitive practice. The problem is data entry.

Japanese word processors have very large keyboards. Until recently, a typical unit had a stack of eight different, large keyboards. Since there are thousands of unique Kanji symbols, converting paper into data was no small feat. That problem can be reduced but not solved by using Hiragana, a second Japanese alphabet of fifty-two symbols. Tell that to your secretary the next time you hear a complaint about word processing. As a result, Japan has been aggressive in developing audio input technologies and devices that convert spoken inputs into digital format.

Audio input devices have been in the lab for twenty-five years, but only now are they within a few years of the mass market. Once perfected, this technology will give the average citizen unprecedented access to information technology. It is one of the breakthroughs that will propel us rapidly forward in the information economy and into a new way of life. While audio input will have many applications, its vital function is to bring the power of information technology to the masses, in the same way that Gutenberg's printing press brought text to the masses five hundred years ago.

Audio input technology holds the potential to do something else that may be equally as profound. Japan's research efforts in this area include real-time language translation technologies that permit individuals to converse in their native tongues through a smart communications medium. This technology would remove language barriers and greatly accelerate the globalization of the economy. Japan's efforts to overcome its underlying linguistic impediments could result in a leading position in audio technologies, just as its difficulties in using telegraph and telex services resulted in dominance of the facsimile industry.

Another potential breakthrough is emerging in video technology. High-definition television produces video images that are a quantum leap better than current television. HDTV produces images that are stunningly close to three dimensional, and offers color and clarity that are hypnotizing. For people who like to watch television today, it's easy to predict how they will spend most of their leisure time by the end of the decade. This technology holds tremendous entertainment value, but it will also greatly enhance video-conferencing, remote quality control, videotex, computer-aided design, telecommuting, and dozens of other activities. HDTV is currently being introduced in seventeen Japanese Hi-Vision model communities. Nationwide broadcasts are expected to begin in the mid-1990s.

Japan's agenda for developing and deploying new information technologies represents nothing less than a master plan for leadership in the global economy. It is actively engaged in building a domestic infrastructure that will form the basis for a new information economy and society. The models, technologies, and institutions that dominate the next era of history may well originate in Japan. Japan possesses the will, and now the resources, to support its new national strategy. Its ability to systematically execute well-conceived national programs may be unparalleled. They are making tracks. But other countries, particularly in Europe, have their eyes on the same objective.

■ Yes, There Is "a" Europe

There has never been "a" Europe, but one is taking shape rapidly. The original Treaty of Rome (1956) established the European Economic Community (EEC) and built a base for the creation of an integrated European economy. That treaty contained a clause which stated that it could be amended at any time by the unanimous consent of the member states. For three decades, not one amendment was passed. The members could find nothing they all agreed about. Progress toward creating the envisioned European economy was slow.

Then in the mid-1980s, as it entered its fourth decade as one economic trading bloc, Europe began to come into focus. Like a young adult that has found his or her calling in life, a frenzy of activity followed. A series of resolutions and initiatives were passed. First, the original Treaty of Rome was altered so that it could be amended by a majority vote of the member states. Then the 1992 Initiative was established with its sweeping effects on all aspects of European economic life.

The 1992 Initiative proposes to remove many of the inefficiencies inherent in the European system. Travelers in Europe today, for example, must still convert currencies when passing from country to country, at a cost of about 5 percent. Border inspections and customs procedures add delays and costs to all shipments. Imagine if travelers passing between Massachusetts and Connecticut had to fill out forms, pay fees, and change money each time they crossed the border. Such inefficiencies have stifled the European economy for centuries. The 1992 Initiative seeks to remove these costs and delays, and promote economic growth. The removal of internal barriers to the flow of goods, services, money, labor, technology, and information will feed an economic resurgence.

The emerging European federation holds great promise, but not everyone believes in it. The 1992 Initiative calls for common technology standards, "harmonized" tax codes, and a coordinated if not centralized monetary policy. Sovereign states are being asked to concede authority for these and other policies to an embryonic central government. Many find it difficult to envision unified European policies, yet considerable progress is being made. Perhaps the most success has come in creating a unified industrial policy for the European Community, focused specifically on information infrastructure and industries.

The cutting edge of the new Europe's industrial policy is contained in a series of high-technology initiatives, the most well known of which are the EUREKA and ESPRIT programs. Each contains dozens of separate projects, typically involving several firms from different EEC nations. The EUREKA program, first proposed by President Francois Mitterrand of France in 1985 as a vehicle for promoting cooperative research in strategic commercial technologies, has since funded over 250 specific projects involving a combined budget of about $5 billion. The program was initially designed to fund projects in three areas: microelectronics and data processing, communications, and robotics. A number of other projects have also been funded, but the principal focus remains in these areas (see Figure 5.1). Several projects have already yielded rich results.

Four firms joined together in a three-year EUREKA project, in October 1986, to develop a European high-definition television (HDTV) technology. The participants in EUREKA Project Number 95—Philips (Holland), Bosch (Germany), Thomson (France), and Thorn-EMI (U.K.)—

Selected EUREKA Projects

Area	Expected Cost (Millions)
ES2: Automated Custom Chip Design	$110
ESF: Eureka Software Factory Automated Software Products	$360
High-Definition TV	$232
EPROM Memory Chips	$450
FAMOS: Flexible Automated Assembly Robotics	$200
Laser Technology Applications	$200
COSINE: European High-Speed Data Network	$300
Gallium Arsenide Semiconductors	$ 60
JESSI: Joint European Submicron Semiconductor Research Institute	$400
Supercomputers	$370

Figure 5.1

aimed to establish a competing standard to fight Japan's powerful bid to dominate next-generation television technology. Within one year, the European consortium demonstrated a working alternative to the Japanese standard, which had been introduced in 1983. The Japanese HDTV standard produces images using 1,125 lines of information regenerated sixty times per second. The European standard offers 1,152 lines per screen fifty times per second. After a very late start, Europe is now in position to compete in the HDTV arena. Contrast that to the American position. With over 250 projects in process, EUREKA will continue to build the technical foundations of the information economy in Europe.

Even greater contributions may flow from the ESPRIT effort. ESPRIT, European Strategic Program for Research in Information Technology, is a ten-year undertaking launched in 1983. It specifically aims at providing Europe's information technology industry with the basic technologies required to compete in the 1990s. The program budget totals about $6 billion. In its first phase, 104 projects were funded in five areas: advanced microelectronics, software, advanced computing technology, office systems, and computer-integrated manufacturing. Each project involves a number of participants from different countries in pursuit of specific technology targets. ESPRIT's submicron semiconductor project, for example, includes Thomson (France), AEG (Germany), and Plessey (U.K.) in an effort to develop state-of-the-art microelectronic processing technology. Another effort, the Optoelectronics Project, involves ten organizations from Italy, Germany, the U.K., and France, and is aimed at developing high-speed optic fiber data transmission circuits.

EUREKA and ESPRIT are only two of several dozen public-sector initiatives sponsored by the European Community. Another effort worthy of mention is RACE, Research in Advanced Communication (Technology) for Europe, which aims to support the deployment of a universal broadband communications "nervous system" throughout Europe. The new network is envisioned to provide videophone, cable TV, data, electronic mail, and other advanced services. RACE will support the design and planning of that network, estimated to involve investment of $120 billion over ten years. There is also a series of programs designed to promote the development of the information services market. All of this says nothing of projects being pursued at the national level in Europe, several of which, as we shall see, loom large on the horizon.

Like Japan, Europe has created a formidable array of technology development projects. It, too, possesses the resources and the will to present a powerful bid for leadership in the maturing information economy. And it holds one critical advantage. Europe is already engaged in an unprecedented process of political and economic restructuring. As Jacques Delors, president of the Europe Commission, says: "The omelette is now cooking. We can't go back to being eggs."

European governments, corporations, and citizens are today uniquely receptive to new ideas. It is as though, having decided to build a new house at this point in history, they feel they might as well incorporate the latest concepts and gadgets. As a result, Europe may move more quickly to embrace the opportunities of the information economy than the United States or Japan. The Europeans are creating nothing less than a new economy and society, and public awareness of this process is a catalyst for change at every level.

▪ Yankee Doodling?

Developments in Japan and Europe pose a formidable challenge to American economic leadership, but the United States is not without its own strengths and resources. American firms play dominant roles in European semiconductor and computer markets, for example. Japanese and European firms have been ineffective in the workstation and microcomputer segments. These machines are built around state-of-the-art microprocessors, and American firms dominate this core technology. Devices like Intel's fourth-generation processor, the 486, still define the leading edge. Other American firms, like Sun Microsystems, have developed their own microprocessors, such as the SPARC device, to power advanced workstations. IBM's RS6000 workstation, introduced in 1990, established even higher standards of performance.

Overall, the American computer industry remains solidly ahead of its foreign rivals. IBM still holds the largest installed base of mainframes in Japan and Europe, and its SNA architecture defines the systems standard in the global computer environment. Japan also lags far behind in the software industry, particularly because of language barriers. Its widely heralded Fifth Generation Project has failed to break new ground in computing architectures, and Japan and Europe still trail in such emerging fields as parallel processing and neural networks.

One measure of progress in the creation of an information economy is the rate of investment in information technologies and services. Investment levels provide an indication of the pace for incorporating new information technologies into the larger economy. Through 1989, Japanese and European firms have purchased significantly less hardware and software than the United States. American expenditures on software and services are not only significantly higher, but they exceeded the combined purchases of Europe and Japan during the 1980s and before. There are more than twenty personal computers in place for every hundred people in the United States, while there are only seven in Western Europe and six in Japan.

The United States holds some other aces. While your HDTV set will probably be Japanese, it's a pretty good bet that the programs will still be primarily American, even if the studios are foreign-owned. The American entertainment industry consistently generates large trade surpluses. The American movie and TV programming industries have been greatly strengthened not only by foreign sales but by expanded revenues from video cassettes and cable TV programming. That momentum should help the industry maintain its dominant position in an increasingly English-oriented global culture. The information economy will only produce additional sophisticated outlets for programming.

Information services and software, the fastest growing and most profitable segments, remain areas of particular American strength. The dominant operating systems for desktop machines, DOS (Microsoft) and Unix (AT&T and others), are American exports. The principal microcomputer software packages for spreadsheets, word processing, data base management, and thousands of other uses are offered by American vendors. These segments are growing rapidly, but software for minicomputers and mainframes still account for the largest portion of the market. IBM alone offers four mainframe software products with more than $1 billion in annual sales. Despite growing competition from European vendors, American software houses hold leading positions in markets for commercial, industrial, and financial applications.

The United States also possesses the most vital venture capital industry in the world. American venture capital firms invest approximately $3 billion annually in high-tech start-up companies. These investments will continue to create new firms, technologies, and entire industries.

Private sector venture capital activities represent a

unique American strength. Traditional Yankee entrepreneurship will not be enough in this competition, however. While venture firms can develop critical new technologies, private institutions and markets are incapable of planning and building the critical public infrastructure needed to compete in the global information economy. Japan and Europe are aggressively building sophisticated public telecommunications networks; the United States is not. While public policies in those nations actively promote development of this critical infrastructure, America lags behind.

Most Americans believe their country owns the world's finest public telecommunications network, but the key indicators tell a different story. Our public networks are falling behind, and *the private sector in the United States is turning to private networks to meet its infrastructure requirements.*

One telling pattern concerns the deployment of new network technologies. Switching equipment is the heart of the public network—all information flows through a central switch on the way to its destination. Several generations of switching technologies are in use today, including the old "step-by-step" mechanical switches introduced eighty years ago, electronic switching equipment that was first introduced thirty years ago, and digital switches introduced fifteen years ago. Each generation dramatically lowers operating costs, expands the scope of services available, and improves service quality and reliability. Today, over 10 percent of the central switches in the United States use step-by-step equipment, a technology that was mature in the 1930s. Less than half use digital technology. By contrast, over 70 percent of France's switches are digital. Other countries, including Canada and the United Kingdom, also exhibit higher rates of digitalization.

Switching hardware provides one indication of public network sophistication. Operating software is also critical. The next-generation network software is called Common-Channel Signaling System 7, or SS7. In addition to dramatic improvements in network efficiency, it provides features such as automatic identification of calling parties. This feature permits a range of functions, including consumer services such as Smart 911 service and call screening. A smart 911 service automatically informs the operator who is calling and where they are located and can provide, in advance, medical histories and other pertinent data to medical teams in the ambulance and the hospital emergency room. For business uses, SS7 opens up a range of opportunities, including the ability to summon data on the caller before answering the phone. Signaling System 7 was deployed virtually nationwide in France in the fall of 1989. That process will not be complete in the United States before the late 1990s.

Incremental changes in hardware and software improve network performance and set the stage for a more dramatic shift. The public network is expanding from a voice transmission vehicle to a much broader set of functions. The next-generation network will carry voice, CD-quality music, data, text, and images, including video. The original version of this new network is Integrated Services Digital Network (ISDN). The first public ISDN trial was initiated in England in 1984, and the first commercial service was offered in Japan in April 1988. ISDN service also became universally available in Paris in 1989 and in all of France in 1991. Less than 10 percent of Americans will have access to ISDN services in 1991. The range of services available is another indicator of public network status. More than 13,000 services are available over the public network in France. The American public telecommunications networks, by contrast, still focus almost exclusively on simple voice service. It will be more difficult and expensive, or impossible, for American firms and citizens to access the advanced features and services central to success in the information economy.

■ IVAN Is Not a Russian Spy

An advanced network drives national economic performance not only through its support of other businesses, but also through its ability to trade globally. The next decade will witness a remarkable new drama in the arena of international competition: *network services themselves will be imported and exported* on a grand global scale. That drama has already begun in the Pacific, and a spectacular show is taking shape in Europe.

In the fall of 1987, the United States signed two international agreements called the IVAN Pacts. This is not the title of a Russian espionage thriller, but a reference to the International Value Added Network agreements signed by the United States, Great Britain, and Japan that permit free trade in information services among the three countries. The agreements, in effect, give these three nations open access to each other's information services markets. At the same time, these nations are promoting new international negotiations to open up free trade in information services on a global basis. But you can't ride the train until the tracks are laid.

The first transcontinental railroad was completed in 1869, initiating a new era of trade, commerce, growth, and westward expansion for the United States. Before then, moving goods across the nation was costly and time consuming. You either crossed the continent by hazardous wagon train or sailed around by way of the treacherous Strait of Magellan. The railway allowed for the rapid movement of goods and people across the continent. At the same time, the completion of a national telegraph system allowed a rapid flow of information and made the Pony Express obsolete. A similar event occurred in April 1989 with much less fanfare.

The first transpacific optic fiber cable landed at Point Arena, California, 3,728 miles from the other landing site at Chikura, Japan. This cable signals a new era in the flow of information between the United States and Asia. In the Atlantic, the first optic fiber cable was completed in December 1988, connecting New York with England and France. The transatlantic cable quadrupled existing information transmission capacity across the Atlantic, while the transpacific cable increased capacity by an even larger multiple. Both cables are already completely sold out. Within five years, however, additional capacity equal to twenty or thirty times that existing now will be put in place in each ocean, and this capacity too will be gobbled up.

These information bridges provide an international distribution channel for information services, and they open a new era of global competition in information services industries. When we call an 800 number today or make a hotel or car reservation, the customer doesn't know or care where the operator or data base is located. That will become true on a global basis. With information moving at the speed of light, the location of the service vendor becomes almost irrelevant. The data base, the information system, or the human operator can be located virtually anywhere. Thus, it becomes possible to export and import information services, opening a whole new series of industries to international competition and a wide range of opportunities to progressive competitors.

In the past, service industries were generally considered domestic businesses that were not subject to international competition. International differences in price, quality, and sophistication of service were essentially meaningless to consumers in most service industries because they couldn't readily access foreign offerings. Haircuts cost only ten cents in China, and you get to keep the bowl, but no one flies to Shanghai for a trim. It is clear that foreign offerings in such industries as hairstyling, dry cleaning, residential construction, local transportation, and restaurants are not readily accessible to most consumers. Now, new service industries have emerged that are potentially accessible to foreign consumers. These include financial services, and financial information services in particular. Insurance policies can be exported, as can brokerage, banking, consulting, and engineering services, data processing, and so forth. We are entering an era in which those nations with leadership positions in the information industry will enjoy opportunities to increase dramatically their exports in a whole new set of markets.

Whenever Americans use their Visa or MasterCard in Europe, the transaction data are transmitted over a private leased circuit back to North America where the information is processed for billing and settlement purposes. The contract for processing credit card charges was won by a bank in Toronto in the mid-1980s because of superior public network processing capabilities and lower telecommunication costs. By the late 1980s, the bank employed several thousand people in this line of business and exported virtually all of its services to the United States. Information service exports are one of the biggest growth opportunities of this decade.

■ The First Information Service Stations

Singapore is a small city state, located near the equator in Southeast Asia. Over the past decade it has implemented a national strategy that focuses on the role of information technology. In 1987, the Singapore government published a document titled "The Singapore National Information Technology Plan." The first page of that document states, "The information communications system is the backbone of the information economy. We must continue to have the best information communication system in the world in order to maintain an advantage in the information age."

Singapore has invested massive public resources in the development of a sophisticated information infrastructure. Today, in fact, the Singapore public telecommunications system compares very favorably with the American system. The technology in place is as good or better than that of the United States, and the cost is significantly lower. That cost advantage has had a particularly important role in building Singapore's position as an information service exporter.

International telecommunications traffic has grown at healthy double digit rates for over a decade, and it will continue to grow rapidly as the economy becomes ever more global. Corporations are becoming increasingly sensitive to the costs of these services. Japanese firms, now expanding abroad at a rapid rate, are particularly heavy users of international telecommunications services. Those services are extremely expensive in Japan. The cost of an international direct dial call from Singapore to the United States averages about $1.50 per minute, whether for voice, data, or fax transmission. That same call from Japan to the United States, even though less distance is involved, would cost almost $4.00 per minute. Singapore's rates are often half or less of the comparable rate of other countries. This cost differential has led to the development of a new type of international trade in the Pacific.

Organizations with extensive international telecommunications traffic, seeing the significant cost savings to be gained in Singapore, are now leasing private lines into Singapore. These firms transmit their international traffic from their home country to Singapore over the leased line, then use the public switching system in Singapore to transmit the calls to their ultimate destinations. In the process, they realize cost savings of 50 percent or more on their telecommunications budget. Singapore is exporting information switching and transmission services. It captures the revenues and employment gains associated with those services. It also captures funds that will finance further investments in its sophisticated infrastructure.

Singapore is today attempting to move beyond basic transmission and switching services to more sophisticated ones. In 1989 it launched a service call Tradenet, which offers electronic documentation, financing, and logistic support for international trade shipments. This service can be accessed electronically by any party to an international trade transaction. It is designed to reduce the cost and time of paperwork involved in the typical international trade transaction by as much as 90 percent. The Tradenet system, if successful, will generate a data base that contains critical information about who is shipping what to whom, at what price, on what shipping line, and financed by which institution at what terms. Within months of its debut in early 1989, several thousand Tradenet transactions were being processed monthly. Singapore is already the world's largest seaport, and it is poised to capture the informational dimensions of the traditional shipping business as well.

Singapore represents one of the clearest examples of a nation poised for success in the global information economy. Its position is built on a sophisticated information infrastructure that provides low cost, high quality, advanced information services. Its success is already quite visible. Singapore today faces only one economic problem: it is suffering from a severe labor shortage brought about by rapid growth in its domestic economy.

Singapore is not the only nation to see the opportunities implicit in information industries. The French have also established a strong leadership position in what they call *telematique*, or telematics. In the 1970s, the French public telephone system was a disgrace until President Giscard d'Estaing initiated efforts to use telematic technologies (computers and communications) to transform the French economy and society. Those efforts are now bearing fruit. The French have developed an information services industry that is unparalleled.

Their information services industry is centered around a public initiative called Teletel, which created the famous Minitel system that today offers more than 13,000 different information services to the average French family and business. Minitel consumer services span a wide spectrum, including home food delivery, electronic shopping, health care, political information, and entertainment services. One medical service allows hospitals anywhere in France to access a patient's medical file over a Minitel terminal. Another serves as a clearinghouse for organ transplants.

One of the most heavily used business services, called Teleroute, allows individuals or businesses to enter a request for shipping services. The customer lists what he would like to ship, its origin and destination, and the time frame. An entry can be matched with entries from trucking companies that list their available capacity, or it can be scanned by potential shippers. Compare that to how trucking and shipping are managed in the United States. Industry experts estimate that as much as half of the trucking capacity on American highways is unused because of partial shipments and empty backhauls. Think about that the next time you're stuck inhaling diesel fumes in a traffic jam.

A recent survey of businesses attributed the following gains to use of services available over Minitel:
• average inventory reductions of over 10 percent

- average reductions in billing recovery collection of 11 percent
- average reductions in travel expense of 8 percent
- average reductions in overhead and administrative expense of 6 percent
- a reported increase in revenues of 16 percent.

The introduction of such critical public infrastructures drives the informationalization of business and society, with all the attending benefits.

Minitel is well established in France, and it is now being exported to other countries. Minitel systems have been developed in five other European countries, and a Minitel-based system has been installed as far away as Brazil. France Telecom intends to sell its services in the United States as well. At present, Minitel services are being offered in Houston through a venture called Videotel, and they are also offered in the Omaha area through a joint venture with U.S. West. Perhaps even more important, with new transatlantic circuit capacity in place, it is now possible for Americans to directly access the Minitel system in France to utilize information services. Foreigners logged more than 40,000 hours of Minitel time in 1989. If you have a terminal, a simple telephone call will give you direct access to a set of English-language services located in France.

While Singapore and France are in the forefront of the emerging information services export industry, Japan and the United Kingdom also deserve mention. The U.K. has been aggressive in reforming its telecommunications industry, with impressive results. British Telecom, the traditional state-owned monopoly company, is being privatized and modernized. The British public network exhibited less than 1 percent digital switching capacity in 1985, but it surpassed 50 percent in 1990 and will exceed 95 percent by 1995. Quality and efficiency have increased dramatically and a host of new services has been introduced. Britain in particular appears poised to capture information service export opportunities, in-transit international traffic, and information intensive business activities. Britain's value-added network services industry, with 1990 sales in excess of $1 billion, is the largest in Europe.

Cable and Wireless, Ltd., the second British carrier, is well along in the implementation of a unique global strategy. With its American partner, U.S. Sprint, it owns the private transatlantic optic fiber cable connecting the United States and England. With Sprint's optic fiber network in the United States, the two companies offer an advanced network that serves all of the United States and the U.K. That is only the beginning. A second transpacific cable, to be completed by 1992, will connect the United States to Japan and Hong Kong. Ultimately, this optic fiber highway will connect all of Asia to the Middle East and the European continent. It will provide an advanced facility that will bring the information economy to the doorsteps of the world. Many nations, however, may not be ready to answer the doorbell, and that list includes several European countries. Telecommunications services were not specifically included in the original 1992 initiative but were formally added in the summer of 1989. That means these services can be freely offered across European borders for the first time.

An extremely important phenomenon that occurs when markets are integrated is arbitrage. Price differentials that exist across markets are quickly exploited when trade barriers come down. A recent EEC study concluded that the telecommunications services exhibited the greatest variance in prices across European markets. A private study found that international direct dial rates were as much as seven times higher in West Germany than in the United Kingdom. That same study found that a standard basket of sophisticated corporate communications services costs as much as eighteen times more in Germany than in the United Kingdom.

Germany and Italy, for example, have been negligent in developing a modern telecommunications infrastructure. The United Kingdom and France, as well as Sweden, have been far more progressive. As European integration proceeds, these nations will rcap considerable benefits from their investment in information infrastructure. Other nations will struggle to catch up.

In the Far East, Japan has tended to be a victim rather than a victor in telecommunications. Its profile resembled West Germany's more than the United Kingdom's. Japan's national industrial strategy has always distinguished between export and domestic industries. Resources and policies were applied to maximize performance in export industries. Domestic industries, those without foreign markets or competition, were never a priority. As a result, many domestic industries exhibit dismal records of productivity and performance. The United States Postal Service delivers twice as many items per employee as the Japanese Postal Service, for example. Amtrak, no productivity paragon in the U.S., reports six times more passenger and freight miles per employee than the Japanese National Railway. The American residential construction industry is several times more productive than its Japanese counterpart, and extreme productivity gaps also appear in wholesale and retail distribution, health care, and food and lodging. In Japan, telecommunications has long been considered a domestic industry under the assumptions that its services can't be exported or imported and that foreign competition was nonexistent. Singapore proved that these services can be exported, and Japan was a principal loser.

The Japanese now appreciate the new status of this industry, and they understand its vital role in promoting a competitive information economy. They have been aggressively modernizing their public network since the mid-1980s. The principal program in this effort is the INS Project. INS, or Integrated Network System, a Nippon Telephone project involving investment of more than $150 billion over about a dozen years, calls for deployment of a modern national network that utilizes the most advanced technologies and offers the most advanced services. The schedule aims for the introduction of three generations of ISDN services within a decade. The first generation, which carries 64 kilobits of information per second, was introduced in Tokyo, Nagoya, and Osaka in April 1988. The second generation, with a capacity of 1.5 megabits per second, was introduced in the summer of 1989. The third generation, called Broadband Service, will deliver 450 megabits of information per second.

The introduction date for broadband service is uncertain, but it is likely that it will begin within three to four years. With broadband service, the full potential of the 4 × 4 forms and functions of the information grid can be brought to the future equivalent of the telephone. Japan and, perhaps surprisingly, the U.K. appear most likely to lead in the deployment of broadband networks. These two nations were instrumental in creating the international standards for broadband ISDN, and they are actively pursuing leadership in what now appears to be the ultimate communications capability.

Leadership in the communications arena has belonged to the United States since Alexander Graham Bell. Even when critical technologies were invented abroad, such as radio and television, they were developed, perfected, and applied most aggressively in the United States. That makes current trends in the telecommunications arena all the more troubling. In essence, *nations with more advanced information infrastructures will enjoy a critical competitive advantage in the global economy for the next generation.*

The best gross indicator of competitiveness may be simply the amount of resources committed to information infrastructure. As we saw earlier, the United States invests more in computer hardware, software, and services than other nations. Unfortunately, the reverse is true in the telecommunications arena. Annual investment in public telecommunications networks in the United States has declined for four successive years, and averages less than $200 per subscriber compared to more than $300 in Europe and Japan. That investment differential ultimately shows up in the cost, quality, sophistication, scope, and competitiveness of information services. Gaps in these areas fundamentally affect national economic prospects. While other nations are aggressively installing advanced public information infrastructures, we are doodling, placing our faith and reliance on a patchwork of private initiatives. After a century of leadership in public telecommunications, why does the United States appear to be shrinking its commitment at the very point in history when the sector becomes most critical?

▪ Too Much *Privacy* in the Information Age?

The United States, in fact, probably invests more per capita in information infrastructure than its peers. But *American investment, per our unconscious yet de facto national strategy, occurs primarily in private, not public networks.* *Business Week* estimated that corporate America invested $14.7 billion in private networks in 1987 alone. Ironically, the largest investor in private networks of all in the United States is the federal government. Its FTS 2000 project calls for construction of a $25 billion private network.

The numbers are reassuring, but the pattern is not. The United States is investing huge sums in information infrastructure, but the composition of that investment is skewed toward the deployment of thousands of separate private networks. It is clear that American firms understand the importance of an advanced information infrastructure. Investments in private networks underscore the critical role of information in corporate competitiveness. Yet the image of thousands of advanced private networks is disconcerting. These private networks are ultimately redundant and inefficient. Even more critically, they are incompatible with each other and can only be interconnected at some cost, delay, and reduced function. And they are private—meaning inaccessible to nonmembers. That may be tolerable in a business context, but not as a social scenario.

More fundamentally, this pattern of resource allocation must be evaluated as a competitive strategy. The American belief in free competition, market forces, and the private sector will run headlong into ideologies that place their faith in national industrial policies and public-private partnerships. Japan's formidable industrial policy machine is being focused on deployment of an information infrastructure. A long European tradition of state involvement in strategic industries also provides a platform for their massive cooperative efforts in this arena.

The United States has been the least inclined to formulate national programs to promote information technologies, infrastructures, and industries. But even the United States has a history of federal infrastructure programs. Government policies and resources drove the nationwide deployment of electricity, telephones, and highways. In the days of unfettered nineteenth-century capitalism, government land grants supported the spread of railroads across the continent. Is it only our current generation of public leaders who lack vision?

New public sector initiatives are appearing. The federal government helped initiate the Sematech consortium to promote American efforts in the semiconductor industry in 1985. The Defense Advanced Research Projects Agency (DARPA) provides billions for advanced research in areas such as very high speed integrated circuits, gallium arsenide, software, supercomputers, and advanced computer architectures. DARPA even played a central role in the federal government's 1989 program to support development of HDTV technology.

Legislative support has also been forthcoming. The U.S. Congress unanimously approved the Cooperative Research and Development Act in 1984, eliminating antitrust penalties for joint research efforts. The Chip Protection Act, providing copyright protection for chip designs, also passed unanimously in 1984, and the Software Protection Act was enacted. In 1989, a number of major bills were introduced to promote information infrastructure development. Senator Albert Gore of Tennessee introduced but has not gotten approved the National High Performance Computer Technology Act, which calls for $1.75 billion in support of advanced computer research and construction of a national high-speed data highway. Gore stated, "Our future economic strength, our ability to provide and support jobs, industry, and technology will depend on our ability to quickly transmit and understand vast quantities of information."

A related initiative is the Federal High Performance Computing Program, a plan submitted to Congress by the President's Office of Science and Technology Policy in the fall of 1989. This plan calls for $1.9 billion in federal funding for advanced computer research and cites the need for a high-speed network to link research centers. The introduction to the report states: "A national high-speed computer network could have the kind of catalytic effect on our society, industries, and universities that the telephone system had during the [early] 20th century."

Recent regulatory changes initiated by the Federal Communications Commission also hold promise. The FCC has loosened regulatory constraints that have inhibited investments in public network modernization. Judge Harold Greene ruled in 1989 that AT&T would be allowed to offer information services over its public network. Both developments will stimulate the development and deployment of advanced technologies and services.

Many barriers remain. The telecommunications industry in particular is overrun with archaic, stifling regulations and procedures. Leadership in the information economy demands positive, progressive policies from both the public and private sectors. It demands the commitment of vast resources. It requires an enlightened vision of the future, and it requires masterful execution of sound, if not brilliant, strategies.

Those strategies must cover each of the underlying technology fields that feed the information industries. They must address each of the cells in the 4×4 information grid. That doesn't mean every firm, or even every nation, has to participate in every cell. As with any strategy, certain areas should be conceded, and resources should be concentrated in areas where the probability of success and the potential return are greatest. But a larger principle transcends individual programs, products, and projects. Singapore and France do not have leads in any area of technology or hardware. They have, however, created and executed leadership strategies in critical areas of the information sector. To be leaders in the second half of this information age, national economies have to become informationalized global economies by building and using the new information infrastructure. Such strategies require visionary champions in both public and private sectors who can see over the horizon beyond the 1990s to the 2020s and beyond.

■ Can't Everyone Win?

The years ahead seem to promise a shift from the arms race to a commercial technology rivalry. There's a big difference. Progress in an arms race inevitably leaves the world in worse shape. Progress in commercial information technologies will improve productivity, bring the world closer together, and enhance the quality of life. Growing global competition will only hasten the progress of the information economy. It is the principal reason why it will have a shorter life than previous economies. That also means we will gain the benefits of this economy faster than any other. Then why so much emphasis on competition? Can't we all enjoy the fruits of this new age through specialization and sharing?

Yes, mutual growth will occur, spurred by competition, and all participants will benefit. But competitive success in this new area is essential to the future well-being of the United States. Building and using the new information infrastructure is not an option or a luxury—it is a competitive necessity. The United States now faces a crisis of competitiveness that could bring the nation to its knees. Continued international trade deficits and the rising foreign debt incurred to finance these deficits pose severe threats. We face an urgent need to reverse these trends by boosting competitiveness. The cutting edge of that crisis appears in financial markets, the most informationalized—and the most competitive—of all economic sectors today.

The past decade witnessed unprecedented globalization of financial markets. New electronic infrastructures provided the platform for the global financial market. In 1973, a group of financial institutions founded SWIFT, the Society for Worldwide Interbank Financial Telecommunication, which permits instantaneous electronic funds transfers between member institutions. The second-generation service, SWIFT II, initiated in 1990, greatly expands the capacity, speed, reliability, security, and range of services offered. SWIFT is available twenty-four hours a day to member institutions, opening up opportunities for around-the-clock services. The sun never sets on the global financial market. Vast sums can be transferred instantaneously around the world at any time.

In the days of relatively closed national financial markets, the Federal Reserve determined the supply and cost of money in the United States. If the Fed wanted to stimulate the economy, it would increase the money supply. It did so by purchasing securities from member banks, thereby injecting funds into the banking system and increasing the money supply. Interest rates would then decline, resulting in greater economic activity. The Fed's monopoly on monetary policy ended in the 1980s. Today, foreign investors determine financial and economic conditions more than most Americans may want to believe.

Foreign investors, for example, typically purchase 50 percent or more of the U.S. government bonds issued at federal auction. Japanese and Middle Eastern investors have carried a highly visible profile in this and other financial markets. British, German, Dutch, and Canadian investors have played a quieter but larger role. Quieter still is the role of Latin American investors, who almost certainly own the largest block of American assets. We are not alone in our own land.

When foreign investors acquire American securities, they are, in effect, injecting money into the American financial system. The money supply increases and interest rates decline from what they would otherwise be. The purchases of foreign investors in the United States in the past decade banished the business cycle. Within a closed domestic economy, natural forces drive the economy along its traditional cycle of expansion and contraction, from low interest rates to credit crunch. In a global capital market, those forces are overwhelmed by foreign investment flows. It was foreign investment that caused the general decline in interest rates, increased real estate values, and led the American stock market to triple in value in the 1980s. And unless the United States can address its continued international competitiveness problems, foreign investment flows will reverse and send the American economy into an indefinite purgatory.

The global financial system is a private sector marketplace. There is no Federal Reserve or central bank to oversee and administer global financial flows. Investment flows follow the logic of private investors, not public policy dictates. This simple fact holds the key to understanding how global financial markets can punish those nations that fail to build competitive economies. Unlike citizens, global investors can call a vote of confidence at any time.

Australia is a case in point that shows the public consequences of private acts in the world of global finance. Consuming much more than it produces, Australia reported an unexpectedly high foreign trade deficit in the early months of 1989. Almost overnight, international investors abandoned Australian securities. But local debtors still needed to raise funds to meet their obligations. That put significant pressure on the limited domestic supply of capital, and the inevitable result was a sharp increase in local interest rates. They soared by 50 percent virtually overnight, causing sharp declines in bond prices and other asset values. Australia had, in effect, been sent to the penalty box by international investors.

Australia had hit its international credit limit. Its massive foreign debt, the largest per capita in the world, became a growing concern to the global financial community. And when an unexpected increase in the country's balance of payments deficit appeared, a deficit financed by foreign credit, many investors went elsewhere.

Australia's economy must now begin to adjust to new realities: higher interest rates, lower domestic demand, slower growth, and the possibility of higher inflation. What is more important, the country will have to begin to service its foreign debt by increasing domestic savings and exports. Significant changes in economic policy and structure will be needed to channel economic activity in these directions. External realities require restructuring of the national economic system.

These same realities hold for the United States. Foreign

credit is essential to the continued growth of the American economy. Over the decade of the 1980s, the United States borrowed some $800 billion net from foreigners. Foreign borrowing continues to grow. What would happen if the United States hit its international credit limit? We had a taste of that medicine with the stock market crash in October 1987. If international investors begin to withdraw from American financial markets, we will witness a dramatic increase in interest rates, sharp declines in asset prices, and negative economic growth. That, in turn, will put severe pressure on the federal budget and create powerful political tensions. If that's too abstract, imagine what would happen to the average American homeowner with an adjustable rate mortgage if interest rates rose by 50 percent. All those buyouts and mergers that are leveraged to the hilt with floating rate debt would go belly-up. Levels of business activity would shrink sharply, bankrupting many. The federal government's interest expense, now running almost $200 billion per year, would sink us even deeper.

This is not just a bad dream; it could happen. In fact, it *will* happen unless steps are taken to restructure the American economy. Either we create a more competitive national economy, or external discipline will be applied through private sector market forces in American financial markets. That external discipline will impose a solution that emphasizes higher interest rates, declining consumption, higher taxes, and severe stress to the business sector. But it doesn't have to happen that way if the United States can build on its leading position in the information economy.

Building and enjoying a leading position in the new economy is a matter of urgency to the United States, and it is no less so to other nations with less extreme downside risks. The challenge to companies, communities, and countries to be active, successful participants in the new economy remains central. Over the next decade, our competitiveness will depend on building and using the new infostructure to support economic competitiveness. If we do not, our economy will weaken and the next generation of American institutions will see their growth stunted.

CHAPTER 6

Between
Molecules and Stars:
Dimensions
of the Next Economy

We wish to suggest a structure for the salt of deoxyribose nucleic acid (D.N.A.). This structure has novel features which are of considerable biological interest.

J. D. Watson and F. H. C. Crick, **Nature**, 25 April 1953

Planet earth is almost 4 billion years old. Animals appeared around 800 million years ago. Dinosaurs lived for about 160 million years, then disappeared about 66 million years ago along with between 60 to 80 percent of other animal species of that time. "Humans" have been around for scarcely 2 million years, homo sapiens for about 250,000 years, and it is doubtful that the species will survive anywhere near another 158 million years.

Everything has its life cycle: the universe, the planet, civilizations, economies, companies, and products. Hunting and gathering economies, for example, existed for hundreds of thousands of years. Since then, the life span of successive economies has gotten shorter and shorter. Agricultural dominance lasted for under ten thousand years, the industrial economy for slightly less than two centuries, and we see this current economy as halfway through its seven- or eight-decade life span.

The completion of the current economy's life cycle is within viewing distance, and the beginning of the next one is likely to occur during the career span of young people entering the work force today. It may well last an even shorter time and be the first economy to live less than the length of an average person's forty-year career.

We can already see the beginning of the next economic cycle. It has even been given a name: the bio-economy. What will it be like? The question is a mix of curiosity and a desire for certainty. Nevertheless, if we understand the future course of our present actions, we do have the potential to create better futures. Our probable next economic life, and the ones still beyond, point to exhilarating futures, but ones that so radically redefine what "human" means— indeed what "life" itself means—that it makes us believe "you ain't seen nothing yet." A popular toast to future generations is to wish them roots and wings. By now, we are well rooted in the near future. It's time to point the way to wings.

■ The One-Minute Economy

Newton's scientific breakthroughs came more than seven decades before their technological applications helped launch the industrial era, and Einstein's discoveries predated the beginning of this economy by around five decades. The scientific breakthrough for the bio-economy began in 1953 with the work of J. D. Watson and F. H. C. Crick, the discoverers of the helical structure of the genetic substance DNA. Less than four decades later, technology has already started to bring the products of genetic engineering to market. Does that mean the duration of the bio-economy will also be significantly shortened? It may pass through its successive stages with greater velocity, but we do not believe that the next economy will be more short-lived than the present one. Although high technology often propels us into the future ahead of our expectations, the opposite is often the case in medical high technology because of testing requirements and governmental restraints.

Companies and industries have their own rules of thumb for how fast they can and should bring products "from concept to customer." Despite the seemingly breathtaking pace in computer technology, for example, a 5-5-5 rule of thumb is not uncommon; that is, five years from concept to prototype, five years from prototype to product, and five years from product to billion-dollar business. It took more than a decade, however, before the transistor made it into a commercial product. It took another decade for transistor-based circuits to get into computers. And they had hardly any regulatory constraints. Non-biotech drugs and pharmaceuticals have a development cycle of ten to fifteen years. So it is not surprising that the biotech varieties will take even longer.

Investors and the public expected too much too soon, even though our astounding expectations may be too modest in the long run. With more realistic expectations, biotech-based drugs are doing pretty well. In therapeutic drugs alone, annual sales are a not-insignificant $1 billion and are expected by stock analysts to exceed $3 billion by 1993 and $6 billion by 2000. Remember, however, that this is for the entire industry, not for one of its drug products. For that, we will have to wait until the 2010s or 2020s, when the aging information economy will make way for the burgeoning bio-economy.

Because the life span of prior economies shrank from millennia to centuries to decades, it is tempting to predict an ever briefer cycle for the bio-economy. But watch out. By this reasoning we would get what many have looked up to: the literal one minute manager!

It makes good copy but bad sense. As much as we would like to streamline clinical trials and regulatory approval, biology and government have natural limits to their flexibility and cooperation. Cancers often take twenty years to manifest themselves, and the results of clinical trials can do little to speed the approval process. Remember how long it took for us to become aware of the dangers of asbestos, saccharine, and the IUD. The five federal agencies that have jurisdiction over biotechnical products in the United States could be coordinated better, even streamlined into one (which would raise its own check and balance problems), and produce clear guidelines. We would still need regulation.

While we are still decades away from even the beginning of the next economy, more important than how long it will last is for us to understand the bases by which it will evolve. Three bases, or core technologies, will have tremendous impact on the coming bio-economy: developments in *mind-like computers*, in *genetics*, and in the extremes of *miniaturization*. Clearly, there are many other important concerns and developments, particularly in energy and the environment, but these three stand out as having the potential to put a stamp on the economy that is just now beginning to gestate. Although some new science is involved in all of them, it is fundamentally the relatively nearer range of engineering breakthroughs that is needed to propel these three into dominant factors in economic growth.

Today, your business may have nothing to do with any of these. But you can bet your business, literally, that tomorrow it will. If your business has nothing to do with genetics, for example, don't think that you don't have to pay attention, any more than you should think that you must immediately jump into the application of genetics to your current business. Neither ignorance nor premature commitment is called for. You would do well to have an early look at the technologies for the next infrastructure, however, and begin now to question how, one day, they will again redefine your business and organization.

■ Would You Buy a Mind Machine?

There are two types of computers in the information economy, and they reflect the difference between the two great theories of physics, relativity and quantum mechanics. These two theories have major and as yet irreconcilable differences that have had an impact on the development of subsequent technologies. Relativity theory is deterministic, meaning that when given a specific set of conditions, precise outcomes are predictable. Quantum physics, on the other hand, is probabilistic, meaning that when observing a specific set of conditions, chance enters into the picture, and predictions can be made only of probable outcomes.

Current computers work according to the earlier, deterministic model; that is, they can do only what they are programmed to do. They don't do very well with ambiguity or approximation. By contrast, the computers that will develop during the next half of the economy will do much better with vaguery. They will make decisions based on indeterminate inputs. Mimicking the way the brain works, they will be able to approximate intuition, judgment, esthetics, and emotions more closely than the most powerful supercomputers from the first half of this age. The first type, the programmed computer, developed in the first half of the information age; the second type, the mind machine, will probably develop in this coming second half of the economy. Moreover, two different approaches are being taken to develop this mind machine.

The first is called *artificial intelligence*, or AI. The metaphor, attributing a thinking life to machines, has stimulated us to build computers that bring the metaphor closer and closer to reality, building on the architecture of programmed computers that characterized the first half of the information economy.

Early on, the prophets of artificial intelligence saw the connection between brains and computers: despite dissimilarities, both are information processors. People like John McCarthy, Marvin Minsky, Herbert Simon, and Alan Turing went to work trying to simulate the brain's psychology, reducing it to a set of formal rules. The rules have no intrinsic meaning. Intelligence and uniqueness, to them, come from the elaboration and particular combination of the rules.

Some of the early rules created an "intelligence" that could play chess or simulate the behavior of a schizophrenic. More recently, the artist Harold Cohen built a program, "Aaron," that creates beautiful and original freehand drawings. Each one is colorful and unique, yet they all have Aaron's artistic style. Aaron has been programmed, but "he" has also been trained. "Expert systems" is a branch of artificial intelligence that emphasizes machine training and learning. It is built on an initial set of rules, increasingly refining a machine's judgments in activities such as diagnosing a patient's disease or approving a bank loan. Despite its advances, however, AI never went beyond these limited applications to live up to its grandiose promises.

The other development in mind-like computers, the one with major potential for the second half of the information economy, is *neural networks*. These computers have very different philosophical anchors. Whereas artificial intelligence is reductionist, starting from the top down with rules, neurocomputing begins from the bottom up, assembling artificial neurons to create intelligence. It is a computing architecture that is closely linked to neuroanatomy and mimics the way the brain works. Its philosophy is to build a machine brain and let a mind emerge.

Computers built in the first half of this economy operate according to programmed rules. When we learn the rules, and follow them exactly, they work. If we misspell an entry, or invert two numbers, the system won't run. Even when it does run, it can never do more than what it is programmed to do. Computers built with artificial intelligence are the latest generation of this evolutionary branch. Neural computers, by contrast, don't use programs, and every solution is a learning experience. They don't use rules but instead figure out the best approximations with what they have in their memories. They are holistic, not mechanistic.

The neural network models perform better than expert systems because, even though they both build patterns as the basis for decisions, expert systems can't handle fuzziness. Neural networks, for example, learn to distinguish a handwritten "1" from "7" and "M" from "N" in much the same way that a child does. This is behavior learned from experience, using context as reference, and working with uncertainty or incomplete information. The memories are built in the form of patterns, in which the current item is compared with others in the memory bank in order to draw the best available conclusion.

Financial services, already the heaviest users of computers, are the first sector to find practical applications for neural networks. Already, for example, they are seeking machines that can read handwriting accurately. Commercial bankers, underwriters, and brokers have a major interest in using neurocomputing to read handwritten numbers and verify signatures on checks and other documents. They are also using neurocomputers to predict stock prices, score credit applications, and analyze mortgage and loan applications. Companies like American Express and Morgan Stanley, as well as many smaller banks, are pursuing their development.

Beyond such relatively simple applications, neurocomputing will be used to build machine vision, speech processing, and general-purpose robots. Each of these is required to recognize patterns from a barrage of unclear or uncertain inputs. A three-year-old can tell a fork from a spoon on a table, although a Cray supercomputer cannot. Neural network computers can learn to see forks, and the Department of Defense would like them to see tanks and submarines. Voice recognition is already in use in security systems and to give commands to machines in factories around the world. Although the vocabularies are already up to hundreds of words, these machines are still learning to differentiate "to," "too," and "two." The Japanese, especially, want to use neurocomputing to develop voice entry for word processing, since keyboard entry of Japanese is so difficult. When voice and vision applications are put into machines, we will have the makings of general-purpose robots.

Artificial intelligence and neural network people are both trying to understand how the brain works in order to build better computers that have qualities of mind. As is often the case in a new technology, different approaches are taken, leading to different architectures, and a battle of standards develops. Slowly, one approach wins in the marketplace, and this may or may not have anything to do with technical superiority. However, the incompatibility of competing technologies may not happen in this case. Current thinking is that both types of processing, programmed and learned, go on in the brain, and, if this is true, then similar compatibilities would occur technically and in the marketplace. If neural networks deliver on their promise, they are likely to complement and combine with programmed computers to create a multibillion-dollar market, including chips, computers, and other hardware and software. There are already over a dozen companies selling specialized neural network computers and software programs. Perhaps more important, giant global corporations such as Siemens, Sony, and Fujitsu are developing neural networks to be embedded directly into their new products.

■ You Need Predictability to Move from the Science to the Business of Biology

Programmed computers and neurocomputers are, respectively, technologies of the first and second halves of the information economy. *Genetic engineering* is the true child of the bio-economy. The ancestral roots of an economy lie in its technology, and earlier still in the scientific principles upon which these are based. This means there can be no bio-economy without, first, biotechnology, and before that, bio-science. Running the sequence forward, science leads to technology only when its principles are understood well enough to predict them. Predictive theory is essential to technological development, and biology is the one science without a predictive theory.

Predictive theory explains not only what has already taken place but also what will take place and why. When we understand scientific principles well enough to predict them accurately, we can use that knowledge to create practical arts, such as agriculture and medicine. Predictive theory is the bridge between science and economy, and technology is what travels across such bridges. When our understanding is faulty or incomplete, however, we cannot predict accurately, and no practical applications follow. Since our scientific understanding of weather is incomplete, for example, our theories of weather are not very predictive, and weather technology as a practical art is very underdeveloped. Technology requires predictive science, and biology is rather new at this awesome task.

For a long while, evolutionary theory, at the macro end of biology, held the most promise of a predictive theory, but it never led to an evolutionary technology. The theories of Eugenics and Social Darwinism were built on faulty assumptions and failed to build a viable technology. Predictive theory is faring better at the micro end of biology. The macro view of evolution asks whether species progress, and to where the chain evolves. The micro view asks how any new species develops. This is where advances in genetics are leading us from scientific comprehension to technological applications. Building on the structural understanding of DNA, genetics started to move from science to technology. The bio-economy is developing by the micro-route of genetic engineering, rather than by the macro-route of evolutionary engineering.

Before Watson and Crick, many biologists considered genetics a dead-end field and, even in the late 1950s, thought that genetic engineering was impossible. Despite such skepticism, the genetic engineering technique to cut, paste, and reproduce new DNA was proven viable in 1973, and gene synthesizing machines developed in 1981. During the next decade, while we are in the mature third quarter of the information economy, scientists and the business community expect biotechnology to advance sufficiently for the next economy to begin its first, embryonic quarter.

The engine for this advance is most probably the Human Genome Project, a $3 billion, fifteen-year effort to map the entire genetic blueprint of humans. In the United States, the coordinated effort is led by Dr. Watson. Britain and France are also current leaders, and Japan, the Soviet Union, Italy, and Canada are also prominent. The two key elements involve mapping the 50–100,000 genes and determining their sequencing. Mapping locates genes along twenty-three pairs of thread-like chromosomes, and sequencing spells out the order of chemical subunits of DNA in any identified gene.

By the end of the last decade, less than 10 percent of our genes had been located. Sequencing, without locating, is like having the detailed architectural drawings for one overpass on the New York Thruway but no way of knowing which one. New advances have been very rapid, however, and machines already exist that map and sequence automatically.

Most gene mapping research so far has not focused on the Human Genome Project but on independent efforts to pinpoint the genetic defects that cause the approximately 4,000 inheritable diseases. Scientists have already identified those for cystic fibrosis, muscular dystrophy, sickle cell anemia, and one class of Alzheimer's disease. Others are being closed in on. The defective gene that causes Huntington's disease, the fatal brain disorder, has now been cornered to a stretch of about 300,000 subunits of DNA near the tip of chromosome 4. This sleuthing is close enough to get the entire sequence, even if its location is shared with several other genes and scientists are confused about its precise location.

When a gene is located and sequenced, learning how its defect causes a disease and then learning how to repair and prevent the disease are still daunting tasks. Gene mapping has revolutionized diagnosis, but not yet treatment. Commercial applications are likely to affect only niche markets for several years. Sequencing machine equipment is an early candidate. Mass-produced diagnostic tests will come later, and designer drugs for specific gene targets later still.

Despite the potential in biotechnology for preventing and treating human disease, it is still not clear whether agricultural or pharmaceutical products will lead the way in the bio-economy. Commercial applications of biotech in agriculture also represent great promise. Genetically modified product groups are likely to include insect- and frost-resistant crops, microbes to kill pests, crops that produce industrial oils and other chemicals, and better-tasting and more nutritious food. Sales of seeds for the four largest crops exceed $2 billion a year, and pest control chemicals are a $15 billion market in the United States. If these are seen as the next generations of product, instead of as a threat to existing businesses, the potential is great. Bug spray does not have the pizzazz of interferon, however, so the business is not as glamorous as human biotechnology. Financing problems, therefore, are even more acute and are slowing down time-to-market and forcing very early industry consolidation. The biotech promise in agriculture is still in the laboratory. Also, reliable new genes still have not been introduced into major crops like corn and wheat. Taste and texture genes still have not been identified, and stockpiling enough altered seeds will also take years.

Livestock reproductive techniques have a history that predates the discovery of the structure of DNA. The first calf produced from frozen semen appeared in 1952. Calves were produced from embryo transfers in the 1960s, and from a frozen embryo in 1973. Currently in the United States, more than 100,000 calves a year are produced from frozen embryos.

Another significant step took place in 1988, when molecular splicing entered the picture, and prize farm animals were duplicated by cloning. The process begins when one prize bull and one prize cow are mated once. The embryo is removed before cell differentiation occurs and genetic material is extracted. The material is then inserted into many altered unfertilized eggs, which develop into genetically identical prize embryos. These, in turn, may be frozen for later use or transplanted into surrogate mothers. The result is genetically identical calves, and the cloning can be repeated through generations. As costs decline and reliability increases, the results will mean standardized biomanufacture of the same uniform quality that the industrial economy achieved in manufactured goods, certainly before 2000.

Fish farming is rapidly moving to all-female populations for similar reasons of enhanced harvest. Farms provided only about 1 percent of all fish consumed in 1980 but supply over 10 percent today, are expected to reach 20 percent by 2000, and may exceed half before we even enter the bio-economy. Virtually 100 percent of the almost 60 million pounds of trout we consume annually are farmed, and almost a third of them come from farms in Clear Springs, Idaho.

The fish farms there expect that within three years 100 percent of farmed trout will be female. Females are better in appearance, texture, growth rate, and taste; males are combative, waste energy chasing each other, and taste mushy. Selected female trout, therefore, are fed testosterone, and produce sperm but remain female. This sperm is then used to produce eggs that yield only female offspring. The idea is to grow the tastiest trout in the shortest time, with the least food and water.

As biomanufacture increases, moral and political questions of consequence will move forward in the public debate. Jeremy Rifkin, one of the most vocal of the anti-biotechnology critics, says "it is a violation of a species' integrity" to manipulate its reproduction genetically. Forty percent of all oysters currently consumed in the United States are sterilized in order to channel all their energy into growth rather than reproduction. The list of such biomanufactured products will only increase in the years ahead.

■ Don't Sneeze; the Machine Is the Size of a Molecule

In 1966, Isaac Asimov's *Fantastic Voyage* was a science fiction best seller about five people in a miniaturized sub who were injected into a dying man's artery to reach a blood clot and destroy it with a laser. A quarter-century later, minus the miniaturized people, these very micromachines are actually being built. A whole new world of micromachinery is also gestating, much of it blended together with the major advances in computers and genetics.

Neurocomputers require new scientific understanding before there will be major commercial breakthroughs, and genetic engineering requires long periods of testing to lift regulatory constraints. Micromachines suffer from neither of these impediments. They involve new engineering more than new science and are put to use as soon as the engineering and economics are worked out. Prototypes of many already have been built, and the abundance of perceived commercial applications far outstrips current development.

Several institutions are involved in microtechnology. In the United States, universities include Carnegie-Mellon (Center for Molecular Electronics), U. C. Berkeley, Johns Hopkins, MIT, Stanford, and the University of Utah. There are big corporations like IBM, General Motors, and Bell Labs at AT&T, and small ones such as Microsensor Systems, Inc., in Burke, Virginia, and Medisense, Inc., in Cambridge, Massachusetts. Government agencies include DARPA, the Office of Naval Research, and the National Science Foundation. Professional associations such as the Fine Particle Society and the International Society for Molecular Electronics and Biocomputers are also organizing the field. In Japan, major institutions like MITI and Tokyo University are getting deeply involved. One MITI proposal, for example, was nearly $70 million for the development of medical microrobots.

What is a micromachine? One micron equals one-millionth of a meter, so micro(n)technology is building things as small as the width of a human hair. These things include microtools, micromotors, micromovers, and microsensors. In 1988, for example, scientists at the University of California, Berkeley, built a working 100-micron motor (two hair-widths) that rotated 500 times a minute. This micromotor was powered by static electricity, not by magnetic attraction like a conventional electric motor.

The laws of physics and of economics are very different at the micro level, and understanding both is necessary to appreciate the dynamics of the bio-economy that is taking shape. When scientists and engineers work with micromachines weird things happen. Friction, for example, is a bigger problem because dust specks act like boulders and moving microtools through air molecules is slow going. Although it is not yet clear what the design limits are, how small things can get, it is clear that small equals tough. At the molecular level a spider's web is as strong as steel. For microengineers, the major occupational hazard seems to be either inhaling the equipment or sneezing it into oblivion.

The basic building block for this generation of microtechnology is silicon, which allows extremes of miniaturization at high quality and low costs. The miniature moving parts are etched on the silicon in a variation of the photolithography that is used to make computer chips. Etched microtools include ball bearings, cantilevers, chewers, cranks, cutters, gears, joints, lenses, levers, pincers, saws, scissors, shears, springs, and valves.

Their potential use is so vast that scale economies would make development and manufacturing costs shrink exponentially. It is said that if car prices had dropped at the rate that computer chips went down, it would have been cheaper to park the car and abandon it than to put money in the meter. We might not get that far, but by shrinking the moving parts and not just the thinking ones, micromachinery could do for machines what the transistor and integrated circuits did for shrinking electronics. If micromachines become commercially viable, their applications will be everywhere: in bathrooms and kitchens, toys and cars, farms and factories, operating rooms and human bodies.

Sensors detect the presence of things like gases, pressure, and heat. Microsensors detect these same things, but in microscopic amounts and places. The microsensors combine microelectronics and micromachines on one chip. A thin silicon diaphragm is packed with resistors. The slightest stress on the diaphragm is registered by the electrical resistance of the silicon crystals and amplified by electronic circuits. Delco Electronics, for example, annually supplies its parent, General Motors, with seven million microscopic silicon pressure sensors to measure temperature, air pressure, and acceleration in cars and planes. The space shuttle *Discovery* has more than 250 microsensors to measure cabin and hydraulic pressure and performance in its main engines.

Another area of enormous application is diagnostic testing, maintenance, and repair in medicine. Microsensors require only tiny samples to produce results, meaning quicker and easier diagnoses. Blood testing, for example, could be done by a pin prick and analyzed on the spot. Researchers at Johns Hopkins made an almost vitamin-sized pill, in 1989, with a combined thermometer and transmitter. It instantly broadcasts, and therefore pinpoints, hot spots in the digestive tract.

Other "smart pills" may transmit information about secretions, nerve functions, and heart rates. If these machines are controlled magnetically by a doctor working an external machine, they could seek out a damaged nerve and repair it. Because of the specificity with which they would operate, they could control individual cells. Again, this requires developments of engineering, not science. They could roam the body, for example, detect cancer cells, and destroy them individually, without having to kill or remove surrounding healthy cells. As we move toward microtechnologies, the human body becomes a space with no limits.

Micromachines have always existed in nature, in cells and tiny organisms. A single bacterium can copy itself in about twenty minutes. Within cells, organelles manufacture proteins in a mechanical way. DNA is a self-replicating atomic machine, and such nature-machines regularly make trees, whales, and people. Today's genetic engineers already reprogram cells to make new proteins. Working at the molecular level, with thousands of atoms, they have created bigger mice and cows that give more milk. Can they get down to one molecule?

Once individual molecules can be isolated readily, scientists believe it will be possible to manipulate them, to build things with them. In 1987, using a Scanning Tunneling Microscope (STM) which is one hundred times more powerful than geneticists' Electron Scanning Microscope, three IBM scientists took a picture of an actual, single molecule. With that event, scientific theory moved from possibility to probability.

The ultimate design limit is to work on an atom at a time and build even smaller motors, movers, sensors, and tools. These are the furthest reaches of those who would bridge science and economy. Their spanner is "nanotechnology."[1] A thousand times smaller than a micrometer, a nanometer is one-billionth of a meter. A typical atom is 0.2 nanometers, for example, and the period at the end of this sentence is about 700,000 nanometers. If the hypothesized nanomachines literally reach the design limit, they are to be assembled atom by atom.

If things can be made atoms at a time, there will never be a scarcity of raw materials, and all manufacture will be on-site from locally available atoms. The molecular computers doing this building will utilize codes, much like DNA, that mimic the way nature has transmitted messages for billions of years. The route to the ultimate small machine might include some combination of biomimetic (from *mime*) chemistry, protein engineering, and STM microscopy. This distant future is where computers, genetics, and micromachinery are one and the same.

These are not the tools of the next economy, however, but of worlds well beyond, worlds where science meets fiction, where futurists and more literal visionaries reside. Leaving them to futurists, and returning to the less distant future, we should try to understand the implications of current realities.

Imagine, for example, a company whose roots are in the refrigerator business. People have relied on some kind of refrigeration for thousands of years to cool beverages and preserve food, such as immersing them in cold water or packing them in ice. In warm climates, people used spices and desiccation to preserve food. Iceboxes were widely used in American homes for seven decades, from the mid-1800s until the 1920s, but they are now antique collectors' items. Mechanical refrigeration has been widespread now for seven decades, since the 1920s. The current technology matured decades ago, and the "white goods" culture of the refrigerator business is deeply ingrained in everyone in the industry. Although few people in the business pay much attention to a future without refrigerators, new technology in the next economy may create better ways to cool drinks and preserve food. In other words, we use the most effective technology available, and when that changes profoundly either we redefine the business that we are in or else we soon go out of business.

Developments in the packaging business during the next few decades may, once again, bring about just such a transformation in refrigeration. Packages and processes are being developed that will give virtually infinite shelf life to consumables. Miniaturization in the next economy might compress the big metal refrigerator to the size of a thin film that shrink-wraps directly around any food or beverage, which can then sit temperature-controlled on pantry shelves. There are cans today that may be stored at room temperature, yet instantly cool the beverage inside the moment they are opened. Smart refrigerators may guide our health by monitoring our intake, the way that smart toilets can now guard our health while monitoring our "outtake." Developments have already begun to put enzymes on a chip, marrying the technologies of the info- and bio-economies. If this succeeds, and combines with the anticipated extremes of miniaturization, then food, clothing, machinery, and any tangible good may be biologically monitored, maintained, and improved. By the time that the bio-economy arrives, the company that manufactures refrigerators may want to be in the food preservation and enhancement business rather than in refrigeration.

Remember, all businesses industrialized during the industrial economy and will informationalize during the information economy. Logically, then, all businesses will use the core technologies to "bio-ize" in the bio-economy. And although we are still decades away from the beginning of the bio-economy, now is the time to understand the bases from which it will evolve.

▪ Redefine Yourself. Ninety Percent of "You" Literally Isn't You

What kind of organizations will develop to run bio-age businesses? In the 1950s, organization models borrowed heavily from biology. Blood as a system, the cell, and homeostasis were all elements of biology used to describe how a business could maintain its healthy equilibrium. The concepts were useful, but only as metaphor, because their scientific base was not yet leading to technological applications, let alone to resulting business and organization.

Scientists are now engaged in useful debate on popular fallacies, such as the notion that evolution moves toward a goal, that the movement involves steady progress, and that organisms can somehow direct their evolution. If or when scientific proof overthrows these ideas, it will also surely overthrow their parallel notions of how corporations evolve and behave. Evolutionary parallels between biology and business life cycles will be reexamined, but with a less self-congratulatory twist. The science of chaos demonstrates how, when using nonlinear systems, ordered patterns exist within apparently chaotic phenomena. And the phenomena are as varied as heart rhythms, rising smoke whorls, cloud formations, and stock market fluctuations. Chance and chaos, not purpose and progress, are likely to guide our economic and organization theories in the twenty-first century.[2]

Since DNA is an information code, the eventual bio-economy model of management may bear some similarity to the models that are evolving for this information economy. In both economies, information is treated as a no-matter thing in itself, freed from its medium and transformed by either software engineers or geneticists. We know, however, that bio-based models of management and organization will not appear until the bio-economy itself is mature. For the middle half of the bio-economy—during its second, growth quarter and third, mature period—companies will run on the by then mature information-based models of management and organization. Consistent with our thesis that models of management and organization do not appear until an economy is in its last quarter, bio-organized firms lie in the very distant, misty future.

It's a pretty safe bet that in the embryonic stage of the bio-economy, organizational forms will be guided more by classical start-up issues than by things intrinsically biological. Less than a quarter of the 1,100 or so public, private, and subsidiary biotech companies are profitable as we enter the 1990s, for example, although losses are getting smaller. Two-thirds of the industry's $2 billion in revenues come from product sales (the rest is from research contracts), and gross margins here are a healthy 56 percent. Genentech is by far the largest and, by some accounts, is worth close to half the total market value of all biotech companies. In the decade since Genentech went public in 1980, only nine biotech-based drugs came to market in the entire industry. Nearly 150 were in human clinical trials and eight were awaiting regulatory approval, the final step before commercial sale. Two-thirds of the companies have at least one product on the market now, up from half that five years earlier, and 91 percent project at least one product on the market by the end of 1991. Despite uncertainties of financing, consolidation, and global competition, the industry as a whole predicts a "tenfold growth in sales within 5 years and 25-fold growth in sales within 10 years."[3]

The 1970s to 1980s ideal of independent and integrated companies, with proprietary capabilities and financed in public markets, no longer exists. Two out of every three biotech companies expect to be acquired in the 1990s, and even more than that number have set up strategic alliances, mainly to finance R&D and to gain manufacturing and marketing capability. They continue to reflect the tension between scientific researchers and venture capitalists with business goals. By 1989 only twenty-nine companies employed three hundred or more people, and these generally enjoyed better capitalization and earnings. Professional managers have begun to supplement, and slowly succeed, founder leadership. The current state of biotech says more about the information economy's ability to support the birth of its successor than it says about bio-age managers.

Bio-organizations are at our furthest reach, at the twilight of an economy that is in gestation and hasn't really begun. Despite how far away this really is, however, we are inevitably curious *now* about what the bio-organization will be like. At this point in time, we can break through to radically different ways of looking at management and organization with speculations. And it is logical to speculate that future models of management and organization may correspond to the science of biology as it will then be practiced.

Most biologists think of different life forms as irreducible entities, but some think that bacteria are the only irreducible wholes, and that all other organisms are really fantastic conglomerations of the simpler bacteria. According to this symbiotic view, plants and animals evolved because groups of bacteria banded together in specific combinations to form them. Only bacteria are really individuals; the rest of us— termites, daisies, executives—depend on our constituent microbes to be who we think we are.

Termites don't really digest wood, for example; they live off the waste of wood-eating protists that congregate in their hindguts. The same is true of people. Although we think of ourselves as unique individuals, amazingly, most of us is not us. Each of us began as a fertilized ovum, which divided again and again until we reached around ten trillion cells as an adult. Living in our mouth and gastrointestinal tract, on our skin, and in various other nooks, however, are *ten times* that number of microorganisms—bacteria, yeast, fungi, viruses, protozoa, and so on—each with its own very different genetic structure and developmental evolution. Either 90 percent of "you" isn't you, therefore, or else we have to redefine who "you" and "I" are.[4]

If our biological definitions of self can be so misleading, it's worth considering that our business-based definitions of organization might be equally deceptive. Our current models, for example, think of the corporation the way traditional biology thinks of an individual—as the basic unit. We have been pushing that down over the past few decades, seeking the smallest viable business unit, something that coexists symbiotically within the larger being.

Taken to its logical extreme, the most irreducible business unit in any corporation is the individual; potentially, each employee *is* a business. Nanotechnology and biomanufacture one day might even make businesses out of our tiniest parts. In the mid-twenty-first century, entrepreneurs might run businesses whose manufacturing plant is located entirely inside their own bodies. Such a view is more congruent with revisionist biology than with the standard brand. Similarly, interorganizational forms will have far greater importance than we have yet accounted for in the way we look at organizations—more corporate bacteria, joining into larger and larger creations.

Molecular geneticists are close to understanding "certain properties of multicellular systems that arise not from individual cells, but from the interactions among them."[5] Applying this type of thinking to corporations leads us to imagine diversified companies that arise not from the growth of parts but from their interplay. Until now, attempts at these new forms have arisen more from social and political philosophy and theories of scale economy than from scientific studies of microscopic entities.

■ Superconductive Management and the Switched-On Organization

Creative thinking about management and organization does not necessarily have to wait until the scientific bases are developed enough to be engineered. They can begin in metaphors, as an almost whimsical exercise, and may lead to a breakthrough that is at once practically magic and magically practical. Using scientific theories to imagine future managerial ones, this kind of playful thinking can be applied seriously to any development in order to ponder its implications.

Although the next economy will likely be dominated by biological concerns, for example, recent developments in energy are amazingly parallel to our questions about organization. Petroleum is the last major source of energy, so far with acceptable economics and ecologics. Barely acceptable. Alternate passive sources, such as wind and sun, have never proved cost-effective, and the public has never completely accepted the hazards of nuclear energy. In the last decade we had two alternative energy entrants, one extremely hot and the other extremely cold. Nuclear fusion and superconductivity, fire and ice, were introduced in the search for nearly free energy. One created and the other maintained enormous energy at their temperature extremes, but each would only be economical if it could be made to occur at near room temperature. Fusion fizzled. Room temperature fusion became the butt of jokes in 1989, but hot fusion is actually the greater fiasco because the federal government spent $8.3 billion in research on it during the past four decades, all to no avail.

We do continue to make advances in superconductivity, however, and if it does become cost-effective, the science and technology of superconductivity could provide a marvelous paradigm for overcoming age-old problems of organizations:

■ Superconductivity

In Science	In Organizations
1. A superconductor is a material through which energy flows without any resistance.	1. A superconductive organization is one through which energy flows without any resistance.
2. Ordinary energy conductors, such as copper, produce some resistance, which is dissipated in the form of heat, an unwanted and unuseful by-product.	2. Ordinary energy conductors, such as managers, produce some resistance, which is dissipated in the form of bureaucracy, an unwanted and unuseful by-product.

In Science	**In Organizations**
3. In some environmental conditions, we have some superconductive materials, but they tend to be brittle and hard to work with.	3. In normal environmental conditions, we have some superconductive managers, but they tend to be brittle and hard to work with.
4. Unexpectedly, in 1986, it was shown for the first time that some materials are superconductive in special environments that can be maintained at almost reasonable costs.	4. Unexpectedly, in 20??, it may be shown for the first time that some managers are superconductive in special environments that can be maintained at almost reasonable costs.
5. The discovery was made by mavericks who "bootlegged" their work without explicit management approval.	5. Mavericks, hypothetically, will have an easier time flourishing within the superconductive organization's fundamental structure.
6. R&D is searching for superconductive materials.	6. We are perennially searching for superconductive managers.

Another example of using scientific theories to imagine future managerial ones involves the fascinating question of how a cell knows what it is supposed to be and do. We each start out as a fertilized egg that subdivides into a group of initially identical cells in the early embryo and then becomes a fetus made up of cells with many specialized functions. How, during this process, did our muscle cells know to become muscle cells and not bone or blood cells? How did the cells in our pectoral muscles know not to shape themselves into trapezius muscles? Science is getting very close to an answer, and as it does the question then also becomes relevant for our understanding of future organization models.

A master gene that determines muscle cell characteristics, "myoD," was isolated by Harold Weintraub in 1987 at the Hutchinson Cancer Center in Seattle. In a remarkable series of experiments, copies of the myoD gene were inserted into several types of cells—such as fat, cartilage, and skin—converting them into muscle cells. The results were astounding, since muscles have an extremely complex structure, far different from the other cells. A family of genes closely related to myoD determines the specialized function of a cell by turning on large numbers of other genes, "committing" or "assigning" cells to specialized roles. In the cells of the early embryo, all genes have the potential to be switched on. Once cells specialize, however, it seems that they lose their ability to divide.

The implications and analogies are striking. In science, for example, it seems likely that someone will try to introduce a myoD gene into cancer cells and stop them from dividing. A similar process occurs in the development of speech. At one year of age, infants have the ability to learn any human language. Only a few years later, when they have specialized in one language, their ability to master other languages closes off. We can use this knowledge to imagine new ways of organizing. Like the cells of an embryo, at the start in each of our businesses and other institutions, members' roles are rather undifferentiated. As the institution grows, members generally specialize, and then their ability to keep dividing slows and stops. If the organizational counterpart to myoD is not present, the organization metastasizes and the business dies.

We see from these examples of superconductivity and cell differentiation that shortly after scientific discoveries are made, and long before they have entered into daily use, we make them into useful metaphors. The metaphors accustom us to thinking in new ways, before we have tools to make the new ways practical. "Turbocharged information," "real-time organizations," "switched-on organizations," and "superconductive management" are examples of this penchant. Metaphors for the next economy are already lurking in current scientific developments. It will take many generations of managers before we have some of these practices, but the very notion stimulates our thoughts, giving us images, if not maps, of new possibilities.

■ Beyond 2020 Vision: How Can We Accept Evolution yet Believe that It Stops with Us?

By the time we enter the bio-economy, we will have accomplished the blending of genetics and computers. This blending will take us in two very different directions: one will be biological and deeper inside ourselves, the other will be chemical and much further away in time and space.

Turning inward, the bio-economy will see *carbon-based organic substances that function like semiconductors*. Computers will enter the body, not like pacemakers and hearing aids that are patched in, but—through microtechnology—like cells that are absorbed and integrated into our bodies. Remember that 90 percent of the cells we call "us" do not have our genes. Microtechnology will add a few more. Scientists do not yet know what a molecular computer will look like, although places like Carnegie-Mellon University have opened centers for molecular electronics. Still, many cringe at words like "biochips" because they raise expectations far in excess of near-term reality. Prototype memories have been predicted for several years but, like the bio-economy itself, have still not arrived.

Turning outward, the bio-economy will also see *silicon-based inorganic substances that have some brain-like functions*. In future economies, we will pass more and more qualities that we ascribe to organic "life" onto nonorganic creations that exist outside our bodies. But are computers the next life form? Dr. Robert Jastrow, the founder of NASA's Goddard Institute, reaches this conclusion in his fascinating investigation into the evolution of intelligence on earth: "The era of carbon-chemistry life is drawing to a close on the earth and a new era of silicon-based life—indestructible, immortal, infinitely expandable—is beginning."[6] In the long term, scientists like Jastrow may be right, but we believe that such an age is many economies away, not in the next one.

Others may be closer to the mark. Roger Penrose, for example, the Oxford mathematician and co-researcher with the famed Stephen Hawking, believes that quantum phenomena are likely to be of importance in the operation of the brain.[7] While he thinks that one day they may explain qualities such as intuition, judgment, and emotions, he views these as attributes of humans and animals, not of computers.

The computing power of today's neural networks is still less than that of a cockroach, let alone an animal or human. In the coming together of genetics and computers, therefore, the brain-like analogy is not in terms of scale but in terms of the way that information is processed using neurocomputers. Computer memories will have more than enough capacity to capture and store as much information as can the human brain. The task for technology beyond the 2020s will be in how the information is processed. In the middle distance, between molecules and stars, the technology of the brain will be one route to our distant future.

The route to the bio-economy will be the micro-route through genetic engineering. Our travels to economies and worlds even further beyond, however, may well be the macro-route of evolutionary engineering. For this, we would have to remove ourselves from the center of things. Then, we might marvel at an extraordinary participation in our own evolutionary futures. Many balk at the notion of non-carbon life. They ask, How can the ineffable qualities of humans be passed on, into computers? In return, however, we must ask, How can we accept evolution yet believe that it stops with us?

If it does not stop with us, and we accept the evolution of beings more intelligent than ourselves, where do they come from? If species do not spring into existence *de novo*, but evolve from earlier forms, then might not humans evolve forms more intelligent than themselves? We seem to think that the apes did it. Aren't we at least as capable as they were of such a creative bootstrapping act? If we admit to this line of speculative reasoning, then we should look to current scientific and technological advances for the likely forms of our future businesses, our future economies, and perhaps even our future ancestors.

Notes

Chapter 1   Just Past Growth, Still Short of Maturity

1. Some people prefer "infotize," "infomate," or "infor-mate." "Info" is also combined with other words to create "infotainment," "infomediary," "infotrate," and so on. None of these, including "informationalize," is very pleasing to the ear. We use it because it is more self-explanatory and complete, even though cumbersome. We suspect that "industrialize" sounded equally unnatural when it first appeared.
2. Clifford Adelman, "On the Paper Trail of the Class of '72," *New York Times*, 22 July 1989, 25.
3. Reported in *Made in America, Regaining the Productive Edge*, by Michael L. Dertouzos, Richard K. Lester, and Robert M. Solow (Cambridge: MIT Press, 1989), 84.
4. Cited in "Will You Be Able to Retire?" *Fortune*, 31 July 1989, 56.

Chapter 3   Find the Turbocharger in Your Business

1. *Wall Street Journal*, 22 September 1988.

Chapter 4   Is It Time to Kill Your Organization, Before It Kills Your Business?

1. Joseph Schumpeter, *Capitalism, Socialism, and Democracy* (New York: Harper & Row, 1950), 83 (Schumpeter's italics and capitals).
2. In an article that appeared in the *Harvard Business Review* almost two decades ago, "Evolution and Revolution as Organizations Grow" (July–August 1972), Larry Greiner described an alternating pattern of relatively long stable periods followed by relatively short periods of radical change. Each long-short pair represented a cycle, after which the organization achieved higher levels of integra-

tion and complexity. In his model, organizations never died unless they screwed up. They always went on to bigger and better forms. Another early treatment of these concepts may be found in the papers in *The Organizational Life Cycle: Issues in the Creation, Transformation, and Decline of Organizations*, edited by John R. Kimberly and Robert H. Miles (San Francisco: Jossey-Bass, 1980).

3. See William L. Shanklin, "Fortune 500 Dropouts," *Planning Review* 14, no. 3 (May 1986), 12–17.
4. Ira Magaziner and Mark Patinkin, *The Silent War* (New York: Random House, 1989), 297.

Chapter 5 **You Can't Ride on Tracks You Haven't Laid Down**

1. S. Umano, *The Law of Technological Civilization* (Tokyo: Kodansha, 1984).
2. Kakuei Tanaka, *Building a New Japan: A Plan for Remodeling the Japanese Archipelago* (Tokyo: Simul Press, 1972).
3. Shintaro Ishihara, *The Japan That Can Say No* (New York: Simon & Schuster, 1991), 21.

Chapter 6 **Between Molecules and Stars: Dimensions of the Next Economy**

1. For those who would like to explore these further reaches, the foundations were spelled out as early as 1959 by the extraordinary scientist Richard Feynman, in a speech to the American Physical Society, "There's Plenty of Room at the Bottom." The acknowledged bible of nanotechnology is K. Eric Drexler's *Engines of Creation* (New York: Anchor Doubleday, 1986).
2. See James Gleick's *Chaos, Making a New Science* (New York: Viking, 1987) for an excellent introduction to the science.
3. G. Steven Burrill and Ernst & Young High Technology Group, *Biotech 90: Into the Next Decade* (New York: Mary Ann Liebert, 1989), 27. Their report, an annual, is probably the best guide to the state of the biotech industry.
4. Physician Lewis Thomas's *Lives of a Cell* (New York: Viking, 1974) is a classic that strikes this chord. The writings of Harold J. Morowitz, molecular biochemist at Yale

(see, for example, "The Ecosystem Within," in *Mayonnaise and the Origin of Life* [New York: Berkley Books, 1986], and of Noble Prize winner Gerald M. Edelman, director of the Neurosciences Institute at Rockefeller University (see, for example, *Topobiology: An Introduction to Molecular Embryobiology* [New York: Basic Books, 1989], are also noteworthy. The work of biologist Lynn Margulis, at the University of Massachusetts, Amherst, has been important here. The cornerstone work, predating the double helix breakthrough by over three decades, is D'Arcy Thompson's *On Growth and Form* (1917).

5. Nicholas C. Spitzer, Center for Molecular Genetics, University of California, San Diego, in "The Chicken and the Egg, Together at Last," *New York Times*, 22 January 1989.

6. Robert Jastrow, *The Enchanted Loom: Mind in the Universe* (New York: Simon & Schuster, 1981), 162.

7. Roger Penrose, *The Emperor's New Mind: Concerning Computers, Minds, and the Laws of Physics* (New York: Oxford University Press, 1989).

Acknowledgments

2020 Vision was written over a period of two and one-half years. Writing a book can be rewarding or a difficult experience, depending upon the relationship that is sustained between its co-authors, and we both wish to acknowledge the mutual pleasure and respect that characterized our efforts. In addition to our co-authoring, Stan provided the original conception and stimulus for this book and guided the manuscript throughout.

The book came into focus during client seminars that we conducted jointly on behalf of Applied Learning, now part of National Education Corporation. Apple provided invaluable equipment and technical support, particularly through Greg Joswiak, facilitating electronic communication between our offices on opposite sides of the country. Jim Routh, Lynné Des Lierres, and Bobbe Glick were very important for their help in the offices, at each end.

Several other corporations and academic centers provided help and haven of many varieties. Sun Microsystems was a meaningful sponsor of the research and writing. Consultation and discussion with executives at Digital Equipment Corporation provided very important help guiding and shaping the book. The International University in Niigata, Japan, the Business Services Center in Perugia, Italy, and IBM's Development Institute in Gavea, Brazil, each provided excellent retreats for thinking and writing at various times. We are also indebted to the Graduate School of Business at the University of Southern California and the School of Management at Boston University for their tolerance and encouragement.

The input of several executives, colleagues, and friends helped us hone our thinking on some of the key themes and on the organization of the manuscript. We would like particularly to acknowledge Mano Kampouris of American Standard, Robert Rochelle of Cambridge NeuroScience, Peter Maurice of Canada Trust, Gerhard Friedrich and Robert Hughes of Digital Equipment, Richard Rowe of Faxon, Barbara Babcock of the Gartner Group, Gary Getson of IBM Canada, Chuck Gibson of Index Group, James Botkin of Interclass, Roger Milliken of Milliken and Company, Peter Granick of Mobil Chemical, Howard Pifer of Putnam Hayes and Bartlett, Marv Standley and Ed Krueger of Southwestern Bell, Jerre Stead of Square D, and Crawford Beveridge and Hilary Rochelle of Sun Microsystems, and David Lee, formerly of TRW Information Services. Stephen Grossberg of Boston University's Center for Adaptive Systems, Brian Quinn of Dartmouth's Tuck School, Howard Stevenson of the Harvard Business School, and Michael Washofsky of the University of Hawaii's Executive Education Programs also gave important guidance and feedback. Joel Friedman, George Gibson, Peeter Kivestu, and William Patrick offered important guidance. Our literary agent, Rafael Sagalyn, and our editors Frederic Hills and Burton Beals were very skillful in shaping the flow and excitement of the book. Thanks also to Daphne Bien, at Simon & Schuster, who was always helpful. To all these people and institutions, and to many others that we haven't mentioned, we express our thanks.

Finally, we are most indebted to our families for their understanding and sacrifice. Bill's beloved wife, Anneke, provided invaluable support during the writing of this book, while completing her own doctoral dissertation at the same time. Stan's dear wife, Bobbi, was a constant source of encouragement, and she supplied many graphic designs and concepts. We wish to thank them and our children, Len, Rick, Hilary, Lisa, and Michael, and Ben, Jay, and Brad, for their love.

Stan Davis
*Chestnut Hill,
Boston, Massachusetts*

Bill Davidson
Redondo Beach, California

Index

About the Authors

Stan Davis is a renowned business adviser, writer, and public speaker. He is a consultant in the fields of strategy, management and organization. He is Director of *2020 Realities*, a Temple Barker & Sloane project implementing *2020 Vision* approaches. Stan is the author of seven previous books, including the influential work *Future Perfect*, which received Tom Peters' "Book of the Decade" award. He is a frequent speaker at public meetings and company conferences on business and organization in the future. Stan was a professor at the Harvard Business School for over a decade, as well as at Columbia and Boston Universities. He resides and works in Chestnut Hill, Boston, Massachusetts.

Bill Davidson is the author of four books, including *The Amazing Race*. The founder of Management Education Services Associates, a management development and consulting company, Bill is also an associate professor at the School of Business, University of Southern California. He holds A.B., M.B.A. and D.B.A. degrees from Harvard University. Bill lives with his wife and three sons in Palos Verdes, California.